THE SIKH HERITAGE
A Search for Totality

(*Previous page*) A SILVER CROWN ENGRAVED WITH *Ek-Omkar*,
PORTRAIT OF GURU GOBIND SINGH AND *KHALSA* SYMBOL
Sikh, Punjab, 20th century, Silver, wt: 478 gms, Acc. no: 90.204
Collection: National Museum, New Delhi

MAHARAJA RANJIT SINGH WITH HIS SONS AND NOBLES
Sikh, Punjab, mid 19th century, Paper, 31 x 18 cm
Artist: Iman Baksh Lahori, Acc. no: 3722
Collection: Govt. Museum and Art Gallery, Chandigarh
Shahib-i-khas Sarkar Maharaja Ranjit Singh Bahadur
(infront of Maharaja starting from left to right) Shahib-i-Maharaj Kharak Singh,
Shahib-i-Maharaja Sher Singh, Naunihal Singh, Shahib-i-Raja Dhiyan Singh, Raja Suchet Singh,
Maharaj Gulab Singh. (extreme left) Amal-i-Iman Baksh Musafir Lahori

THE SIKH HERITAGE
A Search for Totality

Dr. Daljeet

MERCURY BOOKS

TO MY LOVING FATHER 'DARJI'
LATE SARDAR AMAR SINGH
WHO GAVE ME AN INSIGHT TO PIERCE
INTO THE HISTORY OF PUNJAB AND SIKHS

Published 2005 by Prakash Books India (P) Ltd.
1, Ansari Road, Darya Ganj, New Delhi-110 002, India
Email: sales@prakashbooks.com; Website: www.prakashbooks.com

This edition published by Mercury Books
20, Bloomsbury Street, London, WC1B 3JH
for sale worldwide except the Indian subcontinent

ISBN: 1-904668-925

Printed & bound at Thomson Press

Contents

(Opposite page) THE TEN SIKH GURUS
Sikh, dated 1882 A.D., Paper, 33.7 x 46.2 cm,
Artist: Puran Singh, Acc. no: 3787
Collection: Govt. Museum and Art Gallery, Chandigarh

Preface

◆

'The Sikh Heritage: A Search for Totality' is an attempt at transcribing my vision of Punjab. To me what defines Punjab is not a piece of land, a geography or the creation of an Act of Parliament. The Punjab of my vision is a living entity, which has its own life- way and a long tradition of faith, thought and culture and if at all a land, its own colours, horizons, skies, dimensions and character. As acclaims geology, the plains of Punjab grew particle by particle and layer to layer out of the substance brought down to it by its five Himalayan rivers, that is, the plain land of Punjab has its soil endowed with the magnificence of Himalayan heights which its inflowing currents infused into it. So evolved out of its great past, with one of the earliest human civilizations characterizing it, the life in Punjab, its thought, modes, dreams, realities, beliefs, vision, colours, costumes, taboos, sanctions, arts, crafts, tales, songs, symphonies, dance, drama, theologies, rituals, myths, legends, festivals, feats, smiles, tears, pleasures, pains, jubilations and pathos. Different from most lands, Punjab manifests a tremendous sense of continuity born of a massive tradition, which in today's context the Sikh Gurus initiated. This glowing Sikh Heritage, its evolution and role in shaping Punjab, is the focal point of this study. Far above a catalogue of Heritage objects it investigates summarily Punjab's entire past from Indus days to now but more minutely its five hundred years after the birth of Guru Nanak.

It was during my deputation to Anandpur Sahib that I encountered this unique Punjab. In 1999 the nation, the Sikhs and Sikh land in particular, celebrated 300 years of the birth of *Khalsa*. Anandpur Sahib, the seat of the Tenth Sikh Guru Sri Guru Gobind Singh who fathered *Khalsa*, was the venue of the inaugural function for the year long chain of celebrations. The programme schedule included the creation of a Sikh Heritage Museum at Anandpur Sahib and an exhibition of the Sikh Heritage on the occasion of inaugural ceremony. The Punjab Government and the Anandpur Sahib Foundation were jointly holding and hosting these celebrations.

My services were assigned to the Punjab Government for setting up this museum and exhibition. The construction of *Khalsa* Complex, which had to house the museum, had yet not begun. The exhibition, too, was just an idea, a thing to be created almost out of nothing— no appropriate building, no exhibits, and no personnel to man it. Prospective venues were surveyed. The hall of the Khalsa College building under construction, which could be suitably finished, was the option. Workers team was collected from different departments of Punjab Government and the National Museum, New Delhi and put to work. I then toured Punjab from this corner to that collecting objects relevant to Sikhism, Sikh art, thought, culture, or things wherein reflected the Sikh Heritage and the essential Punjab. I was amazed and moved to discover that the faithful ones had been preserving for centuries now the relics, which they believed had once belonged to their Gurus.

It was almost a personal endeavour. I was, however, able to collect and put to display some 300 exhibits that defined the growth of Sikhs' life-way and their struggle and sacrifice for their ideals and identity and wherein reflected the legacy of Sikh Gurus. What struck me most was their unique capacity to reveal the unity and a sense of continuity of life, thought and culture which neither time had eroded nor various pressures or the oppressive hands of tyrants. In a record period the exhibition was set up which everyone said was magnificent. It was inaugurated on 8th April 1999 by the Prime Minister Shri Atal Bihari Vajpayee. The exhibition was on display just for three weeks but visited by not less than half a million people, every viewing eye admiring it and every head bowing in reverence to the holy relics. I was asked to do a catalogue, which was in great demand, but in a hectic and tight schedule with barely two months in hand and a lot to be done it could not be taken up. And, I am happy for this failure, for a catalogue in that frame of time and mind with other priorities dominating, could only be a compilation of hearsay things. Besides, I could not claim to have seen what I had collected for the material vision of an object was not always its underlying inherent truth and this truth I had to apperceive yet.

After I was back, I began recollecting in tranquility, as said William Wordsworth, the known romantic English poet, the 'spontaneous overflow of ' the 'powerful feeling' which had burst into me when one after the other I mounted on the walls these objects revealing the great Punjab, a legacy of the Divines and the face of a living tradition. I began by tracing it across the ages but essentially through these objects or such others, which manifested the Divine benevolence and the efforts of the non-Divine ones wherein divinity sought to discover itself and which sustained and broadened the great tradition. What emerged was beyond the concept of a catalogue and is before you embodying my vision of Punjab best defined as a totality of life on time scale and amidst multi-dimensions and diversities orchestrating them all into a harmony and celestial chorus.

No book is conceived or written in vacuum, and a book like this certainly not. Many institutions and individuals filled this vacuum by their multifarious assistance and I am indebted to them all. I am as much grateful to various collectors, listed on the acknowledgement page, for their invaluable cooperation. For a fuller view of Punjab some subject experts too had contributed to this volume, though all of their articles could not be used. I, however, feel as much grateful to them all. I express my thanks to all others who were always ready to help me, especially my sister Ma Prem Bharti, brother-in-law Atul, Dr.Vijay Mathur, Dr. Maheep Singh, Shri K.K.Gupta and Shri Rajbir Singh. I thank Shri J.S.Anand of Bhai Veer Singh library whose library, a sanctuary for rare books and ready references, was always open for me. I am also thankful to Yogesh and Suraksha, the designer couple, who while designing the book maintained, besides its visual aspect, the spiritual aura of Sikh Heritage and for excellent working relationship I enjoyed when working with them. I am deeply indebted to Smt. and Shri Ashwani Sabarwal of Prakash Books, without whose enterprise the book could not be probably brought out.

My gratitude is due to my loving mother Ma Anand Bharti whose benign smiles and blessings always enthused me to work and made my thorny path smooth. I thank Prof P.C.Jain who strengthened my writing and broadened conception while I was working with him. When editing the book his perseverance, tenability and penetrating skills gave new dimensions to this volume. And, finally I am indebted to Great Gurus whose grace breathed life into these lifeless pieces of paper.

April 13, Baisakhi 2003   Dr. Daljeet

9

Tracing the Tradition

THE TEN SIKH GURUS
Sikh, Punjab, circa A.D. 1880
Paper, 49.6 x 39.2 cm
Collection: Smt. Kumkum Singh, New Delhi

Punjab, the home of the Indus man, in whose endeavors the earliest Indian civilization craved to seek its form and character, discovered itself, on its very outset, in the totality of life, striving to create its own cities, from bricks, windows, ventilators, doors, walls, roofs, floors, drains, baths, alcoves and lamp-stands to a total architecture, and from lanes, roads, public baths, pools, covered drains and community halls to all that could be thought of in terms of civil amenities. It created its own systems, to include engraved seals to trade with, script for storing experiences and sending messages, granaries for collecting food-grains, pans, pots and other utensils for cooking food, storing water and preserving other things to metal casting for manufacturing weapons for self defense and to hunt. It discovered out of its own being, and out of the things beyond, the dance and music to rejoice with, colours to express aesthetic delight and creativity and toys for children to play and learn, innovated figurines and iconographic reliefs for representing its art-forms and votive images and such figures as those of a *yogi or purohit,* and the motifs, looking like phallus, for personifying its idea of the divine and its symbolic form of worship.

A little later, the plains of Punjab, the banks and waters of its rivers, its distant hills, valleys, and woods hummed with the hymns of Vedic *rishis,* but the echoing melodies did not sustain for long, as in them Punjab did not apperceive that totality of life, it appears to have always craved for. Foreign invasions, massive and frequent, began eroding the lands of Punjab. It witnessed a lot of violence, cruelty and oppression, but despite that it fought bravely to its ends, it were neither violent, nor cruel, nor oppressive. Punjab sought itself in courage and formidability but was never characterized as a land of mere warriors. It embraced element of passion and emotion, its fields, meadows, skies and horizons resounded with melodies of forgotten love, separated friends, pangs of departed ones, and pain and pathos, and it danced to a rhythm, and boisterously, to the jubilation of exuberant hearts around the heap of harvested crop, or around a camp-fire, yet Punjab did not seek to identify itself in dance or music, in romance or love, in song or sorrow, in jubilation or pathos, or in blood or emotion.

The soil of Punjab essentially sought itself in balance, harmony and synthesis. The multiplicity rather than the absoluteness of life, was more akin to Punjab. As had Indus shaped its earliest life, its rivers seem to have always shaped its vigorous multiplicity. Like these rivers it streamed, slow or fast, in lean summer ripples or in mighty monsoon floods, well within its bounds, or beyond, superceding them sometimes, but conceding finally to their authority, across both, the sterile expanse of sands and the affluent lands.

The cult of life in Punjab had, thus, its earliest roots in the wholeness of the Indus life. Different from a tradition of thought, theology or rituals, or that of literature, arts, or music, or of romance, chivalry or sacrifice, Punjab discovered itself in life's totality, instead of any of its excellences, and in man, rather than in individuals. And, it was perhaps in tune with this spirit of the soil of Punjab that the Sikh Gurus sought their Sikhs and themselves to merge into their role and deeds, and the individual was thus institutionalized.

Whatever its distant past, roots or inspirations, the globally known Punjab of the day appears to have a past receding to just some five hundred years or so, when a mighty tradition was born or re-born. It was essentially born of Guru Nanak's spiritualism consisting of both, theology and

SERPECH — A STUDDED ORNAMENT USUALLY WORN OVER THE TURBAN
Sikh, Punjab, early 19th century, 22 x 12.5 cm, Acc. no: 87.1166
Collection: National Museum, New Delhi.
*This beautifully designed serpech is set with diamonds in
gold and is delicately enamelled on reverse.*

12

devotion. It encompassed within it his ethical consideration revering individual goodness as the essence of the universal goodness, his humanism emphasising casteless creedless love, fraternity and equality as man's supreme attributes and his socialism requiring all to meet, communicate, pray and feed together for knowing the mankind better, developing restraint and self-discipline and love for each other and for mutually realizing **Him**. Nanak's tradition sought to institutionalize authority, the Guruship in his own case, which imparted to it unity, impersonality and perpetuation, aiming at building a good individual, better society and a stronger nation.

With Guru Nanak's tradition was conceived a new manhood, new society and a new nationhood. This newly conceived man was Guru Nanak's Sikh, the creation of this tradition, neither better nor worse, but essentially different. Superiority, or supremacy, was never aimed at, or even favoured, for in Nanak's tradition, which strove otherwise at equalizing all, and at discovering the individual in his impersonal role, no one, whosoever, the Guru or the Sikh, had a place either below or above others.

(Opposite page) PORTRAIT OF GURU NANAK
Sikh, Punjab, circa A.D. 1870-75
Paper, 36 x 28 cm, Acc. no: 2401
Collection: Govt. Museum and Art Gallery, Chandigarh.
Guru Nanak's choga inscribed with Japuji and Quranic verses in Persian.

The Divine Masters

Guru Nanak

Sat Guru Nanak pargataya, miti dhundha jag channan hoya

Guru Nanak, the first Guru of Sikhs and the creator of the new tradition, born in 1469 at Rai Bhoe-ki-Talwandi, now Nanakana Sahib, in Pakistan, was predicted on his birth to lead both Hindu and Musalman to new path. As predicted, he showed exceptional interest in cosmic questions and fundamentals of life when yet a child. His father Mehta Kaluchand, an orthodox Bedi, sought to keep his son's interests centred to formal learning arithmatics, accountancy, Devanagari, Persian and Arabic, but this hardly changed child's mind from spiritual bent. As an unfailing remedy to keep along the worldly path his father married him in 1487 to a girl Sulakhni. She bore him two sons, but despite, Nanak's outlook was not changed.

For her strained father's relief, Nanaki, Nanak's elder sister, took him to Sultanpur where her husband, Jairam, managed for him storekeeper's job at Daulat Khan Lodi's *Modikhana*. But destiny had for him at Sultanpur something different. There he met Mardana, a Muslim minstrel *mirasi* who could spell-bound people when he played on *rabbab*. Though ten years older to Nanak, Mardana was immensely fascinated by his melodious voice, charming manners, emotional verses and ideals of love for humanity. He joined Nanak in insepa-

rable unity as his first disciple and companion. Now onwards every corner and public square began rebounding with Nanak's songs and Mardana's *rabbab*.

Nanak was now thirty. He had been at Sultanpur for seven years. Every morning he went to the local river for his daily bath. One morning he did not return. When searched, he was found missing,

though his clothes lay on the river-bank. Everybody concluded that he had drowned. But he re-appeared the third day. He was set deep within him and his face glowed with a unique brilliance. He was now an Enlightened One. He kept introspecting the whole day. The next morning he re-iterated the principle of universal brotherhood:

(Top) Guru Nanak with his teacher Gopal Pandit
(Above) Guru Nanak in service at Daulat Khan Lodi's stores
Sikh, Punjab, circa. A.D. 1900, Paper, 42 x 30.5 cm
Artist: Lahora Singh, Acc. no: P/55-3, 10
Collection: Patiala Archives, Patiala

14

'Nai koi Hindu na koi Musalman', and, with it advanced his vision of harmony, tolerance and unity. It contemplated entire mankind as one whole and paved way for soul's ultimate union with the Supreme. Having given up his job and all belongings away to needy ones, he was now a *faqir*, travelling from one holy place to the other, from one of the Hindus to the that of the Muslims, or the Jain or the Buddhist, within the country and beyond.

As has been conceived in artistic vision, he had a glowing face with a halo around, a saffron mark on his forehead, a conical *qalandari topi* on head, a garland around his neck, a rosary in hand and a *faqir* like *jama* on his person. Mardana accompanied him constantly. Broad-based was his vision, mystic his appearance, convincing his arguments, spirited his songs and as much Mardana's *rabbab*. Wherever he went, he converted many to his ideals, and all into his admirers. His first formal disciple, the Sikh, was Bhai Lalo, a carpenter from Sayyidpur in Gujranwala, now in Pakistan, a place he had chosen to begin his itinerancy. He travelled to Sialkot thenafter and met the known saint Shah Hamzah and to Achal Batala, and discoursed on theological matters with *yogis* and wise ones gathered there on *Shivaratri*.

At Talwandi he went to pay respects to his parents and on the way to Multan halted for sometime at Chhanga Manga forest to meditate, and at Chuniana to meet Sheikh Daud Karamati and Sayyid Hamid Ganj Baksh. The saints at Multan sent him a bowl filled with milk to its brim suggesting that Multan already had many saints leaving him no place. Nanak sent back the bowl with a jasmine flower afloat indicating that his fragrance-like presence would only add fragrance to Multan's life. Here he met Sheikh Ibrahim and the head of Baba Farid's shrine. He reformed the notorious Sajjan *thag*, and by converting into a *dharmashala* the house he donated, established God's ever first abode for commemorating **His**

NAWAB DAULAT KHAN LODHI LOOKING FOR GURU NANAK
BELIEVED TO HAVE DROWNED IN RIVER VAHI
Sikh–Pahari mix style, early 19th century
Paper, 18 x 15.5 cm, Acc. no: 63.132
Collection: National Museum, New Delhi.

SHESH-NAGA UNFURLING ITS UMBRELLA LIKE A HOOD OVER GURU NANAK
Pahari–Sikh mix style, early 19th century
Paper, 16.5 x 15.5 cm
Collection: S.S. Hitkari, New Delhi.
The artist has attributed Vishnu-like divinity to Baba Nanak by
associating with him the emblem of serpent, obviously,
Shesh, a traditional accompaniment of Vishnu.

16

(Opposite page) GURU NANAK WITH BHAI MARDANA AND BALA
Sikh–Pahari mix style, Punjab, mid 19th century
Paper, 23 x 17 cm, Acc. no: D/32
Collection: Sheesh Mahal Museum, Patiala.
It is a fully evolved portrait of Guru Nanak as it is endowed with most of the symbols usually
associated with him and are now a well established tradition.
Alike the serenity characterizing his very being is seen emerging here in the treatment of his face, posture and demeanour.

name. On his way back, he visited Pakpattan and Baba Farid's seat at Dipalpur.

For twelve years he was in eastern part, visiting Kurukshetra on solar eclipse ablution, Mathura, Vrindavan, Agra meeting saints, *faqirs*, holy ones, *pandits* and *maulavis* teaching the great ideals of love, truth, honesty and inward purity. The rigid authority sometimes felt offended as at Kuruksheta imprisoning him and Mardana but when they began converting the very atmosphere of jail by their hymns and music it preferred to set them free. At Kamrup, Nur Shahi, the known conjurer, tried to infatuate Baba Nanak by her extraordinary tempting charms, but her ignorance was shedded off the moment compassionate Nanak sang to her a hymn now known as *Kuchchaji*. She fell at his feet and dedicated to Nanak's path. Kabir *panthis* claim Nanak's meeting with Kabirdas at Varanasi and Vaishnavites his meeting and dancing with Chaitanya at Jagannathpuri. On his way to Talwandi he visited most of the major towns in central India.

He later went to south upto Rameshwaram and Sri Lanka. On his route fell Tamilanadu, Andhra, Central India and Rajasthan. In Rajasthan he had opportunity to meet Mirabai, the great poetess and a saint senior in age. While coming back to Sultanpur he chose a different route covering

Kerala, Mysore, Maharashtra, Gujarat and Sind. In Gujarat he met known Vaishnava saint Vallabhacharya. When 46, he headed towards north and was in Himalayan region for two years. He met *yatis, sadhus* and held discourse with followers of Nath sects of Gorakhanath. All were highly impressed with Nanak's mission journeying to unveil truth that darkness of falsehood enshrouded.

Guru Nanak went last to Mecca and Madina in west Asia. While asleep, his feet unconsciously turned towards *Ka'aba*, the holy shrine. A *qazi* come to pray felt offended. He protested Guru Nanak of showing disrespect to God's house. Quietly came Nanak's answer, "please turn my feet to the direction where the all pervading God in not present." *Qazi* was bewildered to see *Ka'aba* wherever he turned Guru Nanak's feet. As mentions Bhai Gurdas, Guru Nanak also went to Baghdad with Mardana. On his way back he was for some time at Hasan Abdal with Vali Qandhari. When questioned about his faith at Madina, he reiterated in Kabir's words his humanism "if I say Hindu, I risk my life, I am also not Musalman; I am a thing of five elements wherein lives God"

Hindu Kahan tan mariyon,
Musalman bhi nanh,
Panch tatva ka putla, ghebhi khela manh

While wandering from a shrine to a saint, a mosque to a *maulavi*, *Sufi* to a *sanyasi*, Guru Nanak craved to know why there was suffering when the land had thousands of temples, sacred *thirthas*, holy men, age old religion, teachings and traditions. He felt mankind needed most to practise equality and fraternity, the highest principles of living, and commemorate His **Nam,** the most effective instrument of spiritual elevation and communion of self with the Supreme. Hence, with whatever he had known he decided to settle down and preach. Nanak's penetrating wit, unique wisdom and tolerance which greatly influenced all, *pandas* at Haridwar, *pandits* at Banaras, *mullas* at Mecca and *pirs* at Baghdad, were now ever more effective converting to his path all who came in his touch. This dedication to **His Nam**, a path independent, quite new and simple, which Guru Nanak initiated, was known as *Nam marg,* or *Simran marg*. It introverted vision from beyond to within and opened the all-viewing window inside, for Nanak believed that the Beloved One was not far from him who sought **Him** within himself. Besides, communion of self with the Supreme by *simran* led the individual to God's constant companionship. Near the holy river Ravi, on land donated by

Diwan Karorimal Khatri, Guru Nanak established his humble seat giving it **Kartar's** name, Kartarpur, the abode of the Creator, the all-Doing.

In God's devotion consisted Nanak's mysticism, a thing plain and simple, clear and precise. He asserted there was but one God, all-creating, all-doing, true, un-born, immortal, self-existent and beyond fear, enmity and all passions. He did not approve the idea of God's incarnation as the human form, or anyone born, was subject to decay and death, whereas his *Karta Purakh* was *Akal*, the timeless, and as such a formless existence for no form was beyond time. His God, the true lord, was *Sat*, the true, and was in existence before anything came into being, or time began spanning universe. He was both immanent and transcendental. This *Akal Purakh* of Guru Nanak was *Sat, Karta* and *Saibhanga*, the one who was never born was yet always in existence. His brief and simple *Mul mantra 'Ek-Omkar'*, meaning 'there is one God', contains not only his concept of God but also the gist of his mystical experiences related to truth and salvation. As elaborated in *Japuji* it asserted:

*"He is One,
His name is Truth, the Creator,
He knoweth not fear or hatred;
He is beyond time, immortal,
His spirit pervades the universe;*

*He is not born, nor does
He die to be born again,
He is self-existent,
By the Guru's grace
Thou shalt worship Him,
God is Nirankar, the formless."*

His communion, different from earlier modes of devotional gatherings and assemblies, comprised of *sangat* and establishments like *dharmashala* and *pangat* or *langar*, where his disciples regularly met to elevate themselves spiritually by singing in **His** praise and to strengthen the bonds of humanism, the equality and fraternity, by eating together as one united whole. Guru Nanak insisted upon personal goodness and self-discipline, as it was in them that the religion of an individual got expressed. He believed from good individual living emerged a good society. Unlike other theologists whose concern remained restricted to mere individual, in Nanak's concept building of a good society and thereby a good nation was as much important as the elevation of an individual. Though *Khalsa*, a people with a difference in life-style and thought, came into being some two hundred years after Guru Nanak, yet the seeds for a section of people, mostly his Sikhs, to grow into a different and one of the most powerful communities of man had been laid in the *sangat*

and *pangat* aspects of Guru Nanak's teachings for his Sikhs.

Guru Nanak neither practised nor taught renunciation for he believed that house-holders could do within their own fold whatever was required for their spiritual upliftment, or their communion with the Supreme, and also help build a better society and stronger nation. Initially conservative *yogis* approved it not. One *yogi* Bhagandarnath sarcastically questioned him as to why he mixed acid with milk. He disapproved that a holy man, as acclaimed Guru Nanak to be, led a family life. Guru Nanak calmly said that Bhagandarnath, considering the family life impure, had renounced it so that he could lead a pure life, but despite he went to houses of family men to beg. He asked Bhagandarnath how would the purity sustain and prevail on food that householders contributed, if the household bred only impurities. He wanted Bhagandarnath to appreciate that one could abide pure amid the impurities of the world as Bhagandarnath could breed purity despite when fed by impure household. This to a great extent explains how in Guru Nanak's path renunciation was irrelevant.

The supreme bliss, a state of mind, which knows neither pleasure nor pain, was the highest goal he set before his disciples to strive for. He considered *Simran* of the true **Nam** as the highest

and the purest form of worship and the most effective instrument of God's realization. He commanded his disciples to devote to the true **Nam**, which, he said, removed all obstacles to salvation. He often said, "I have no miracles save his true **Nam**". Like Kabir he compared the intensity of a devotee's *bhakti* or devotion, and loving adoration for meeting his true Lord with the yearnings of a bride pining to unite with her spouse. Complete detachment from everything else and desiring God with complete dedication and by all faculties was the purest form of *bhakti*. Guru Nanak was convinced that *bhakti* found expression in *sarvana*, the listening, *pad-sevana*, the worship of feet, *archan*, the offering, *vandana*, the prayer, *das-bhava*, the total submission, *maitri-bhava*, the friendship, and *atma-nivedan*, the eradication of ego. The door to salvation opened by God's *nazaar*, *kirpa*, *parsad* and *daya*, various forms of **His** grace, and *dan*, the charity, *isnan*, the ablution, *seva*, the service, and *simran*, the prayer, were the means of **His** realization. Guru Nanak's entire life was devoted to preaching **His Nam**. He believed that commemorating **His Nam** with the singleness of mind, the subtlest instrument of **His** realization, brought God's grace.

The personalness of the Hindu God, the spiritual equality of Buddhism and congregation of

Islam were all combined in Guru Nanak's Sikhism. He was a Prophet of the same magnitude as were Lord Buddha, Jesus Christ and Muhammad Sahib. He showed the path of **Nam** *simran*, which illuminated even the darkness. Conceived beyond the narrow barriers of caste, race and geography he perpetuated a path of material and spiritual upliftment, which was open to all alike. His religion was more or less universal and secular. The slogan, which he gave *'Na koi Hindu, Na koi Musalman'*, represented his humanism, vision of harmony, tolerance and man's co-existence and his ultimate union with the Divine. *Gurmat*, or Guru's vision, was the name, which he gave to his *Panth*.

Guru Nanak was an exceptionally sensitive poet. Learned controversies, which the theological abstractions usually involved, little engaged him. His poetry, with the simple lucid manner of its composition, the commonness of its theme collected mostly from man's every day experience, and the unique lyrical flavour which its language was endowed with, and above all his simple spiritualism appealed primarily to heart. Guru Nanak was man's great friend, ocean of mercy, healer of sinners, cherisher of poor and destroyer of sorrow. He was wise, generous and bountiful and a kind of divine charm crowned his entire being.

22

TOKEN OF GURU NANAK
Sikh, Punjab, early 19th century
Gold, Dia: 2 cm, Acc. no: 65.497
Collection: National Museum, New Delhi.
Obverse: Baba Nanak with Bala and Mardana
Reverse: 'Mool Mantra' of Japuji Sahib.

Guru Angad

Ji jant sab sarni tumhari, sarb chint tuj paase,
Jo tuj bhave soi changa, ek Nanak ki ardase

GURU ANGAD
Guler, Pahari, circa A.D. 1800
Paper, 26 x 22 cm, Acc. no: F-40
Collection: Lahore Museum, Lahore, Pakistan.

GURU ANGAD PAYING HOMAGE TO BABA NANAK
A folio of Janam Sakhi
Sikh–Pahari mix style, Punjab, circa A.D. 1800
Paper, 18 x 15.5 cm, Acc. no: 63.1325
Collection: National Museum, New Delhi.

Guru Angad Dev, the second of Sikh Gurus, was the chosen one to receive and perpetuate Guru Nanak's legacy, a tradition which bred a truer man, a better society and a stronger nation using love, equality, fraternity and devotion as its soul, *sangat* and *pangat*, devotional congregation, music and song, poetry's emotional appeal and *simran* of **His Nam** as its operative body and the communion with the Supreme, **His** realisation, as the ultimate goal of all created ones. The very name Angad which Guru Nanak gave to his chosen Sikh Lahina suggested that the great Guru considered him part of his own being and the one who could carry the torch to the farthest end.

After Guru Nanak knew that the great extinction was close, just twenty days before his *Nirvana* on 7th September 1539 he held a congregation of his Sikhs. Amid thousands his eyes rose and fixed at Lahina, one of his two beloved Sikhs who had joined him at Kartarpur, the other being Buddaji, popularly know as Baba Buddaji, who had a long tenures of life gaining him honour of applying *tilaka* to five of the ten Sikh Gurus. He summoned Lahina to dais and placed at his feet his head and five paisa and a coconut as his offering to the new Sikh Guru. Guru Nanak then gave to the new Guru

the *Bani-pothi*, a collection of his own life-time hymns and poems, and a rosary, the symbols of his legacy, and called him by the name Angad, a part of his own being. Suggestively he acclaimed that Angad shared his entire being, his deeds, divinity, vision and thought and all his aspirations

and objects. And, Guru Nanak had thus institutionalized the Guruship imparting to it unity and perpetuation, a sort of impersonality beyond individualistic existence, indivisibility and continuity.

Lahina was born on 3rd March, 1504 at Harika, a small village in Firozpur district of Punjab

24

(Opposite page top) KUNDA(RING) OF A BROKEN *LOH*(PAN)
USED FOR BAKING *CHAPPATIS* FOR *LANGAR*
Collection: Baba Farid Museum, Faridkot, Punjab.

(Opposite page bottom) MATA KHIWI PREPARING *LANGAR*
Mata Khiwi, the consort of Guru Angad, was the first woman in Sikh Panth
to participate actively in Panth's activities. It was she who institutionalised
langar as a sacred organ of the Panth imparting to it divine sanctity.

to a Khatri trader Pheru, popularly revered as Bhai Pheru. He was a devotee of Goddess Durga. One day when passing across a lane he heard an enchanting melody sung in an equally bewitching voice. Spell bound Lahina was drawn to the person who sang it.The infatuated Lahina was Bhai Jodha, a disciple of Guru Nanak. Fully absorbed he was reciting Guru Nanak's *Asa-di-var*. A determination crept in Lahina's mind. With a sort of compulsion to have a vision of the creator of the great melody he to set out in his search. His all time companion Budda too joined him. He reached Kartarpur and was aface the great Master. And, as acclaim unanimously all sources, Lahina was completely transformed into a new being the moment the great Master cast at him his ever first glance. There are many who believe that the great Guru had implanted into Lahina's person his own being that very moment and had nominated him his torch bearer, the courier of his spiritual legacy. To such ones Lahina had been transformed into Angad when he first encountered the great Master.

Guru Angad, before he passed away in 1552, had a small tenure of just 13 years to work with Guru Nanak's legacy; he, however, carried it forward both in letter and spirit. He mainly emphasized on preserving and carrying to a larger community of people Guru

Nanak's *Bani* and thereby converting them to Nanak's great path of *Nam-simran*. Prior to him Guru Nanak's hymns were either inscribed in the script known as *Lande-Mahajani* or contained in his disciples' memory. With no vowel sound this script was rather crude and lacked in uniformity. Guru Angad, in his effort to make it uniform and more communicative, added to it vowels, fixed consonant sound and introduced intonations and linguistic structures and thus revised it to a simpler and more uniform vehicle of lingual expression. This revised script of Guru Angad came to be known as *Gurmukhi*, something emitted from Guru's own throat, or mouth. Guru Angad, the originator of the script of *Gurmukhi*, recorded in this new script Guru Nanak's all hymns contained in either traders' ledgers or in people's memory. Pursuing the great spiritual and literary tradition laid by Guru Nanak, Angad added to the *bani* some hymns of his own. This tradition of compiling earlier Gurus' *bani* by the succeeding Guru and adding to it his own, the nucleus of Sikh faith and the root of the Sri Guru Granth Sahib concept, was Guru Angad's contribution to the Sikh Panth. The *bani* of Guru Angad, compiled in chaste *Gurmukhi* in simple, direct and effective manner was superb in poetic essence and brimmed with exceptional

wisdom. It imparted the message that the path to liberation could be sought only by the grace of Guru. Later, when Sri Guru Granth Sahib was compiled, the holy Book included 63 *salokas* of Guru Angad, each a gem of wisdom.

The concept of *langar*, or *Guru-ka-langar*, as it came to be known by Guru Angad's days, a sort of community kitchen, was further consecrated and widened. It was run with offerings that devotees and visitors made, but was looked after directly by Guru's wife Mata Khiwi herself, giving it the sanctity of a divine institution. Thus, this instrument of social communion, the *langar*, operating beyond consideration of caste, creed or status, was made the pioneer spiritual institution of Sikhism. It bred amongst Sikhs a feeling of social equality and kept them united as one single whole. *Sangat*, the spiritual gathering where disiciples met their Guru and commemorated with him **His Nam**, had now greater sacredness and become the supreme form of worship. *Jap, tap, sanjam,* and *kshama,* the meditation, austerities, abstinence and forgiveness, were subtler instruments of *sangat* to be observed alike both by the Guru who embodied them and the disciples who strove for them for the *sangat* in its very concept prescribed *sangati*, a common course, during the life and thereafter for all persons alike.

Guru Amardas

Satguru ka updesh suni tu hove tere nale
Kahe Nanak man piyare tu sada sach samale

GURU AMARDAS AND HIS SOCIAL REFORMS
Sikh, Punjab, Modern, Oil on canvas, 30" x 40"
Artist: Devender Singh, 1978
Collection: Punjab and Sind Bank, New Delhi.
This painting in its three compartments depicts very powerfully
and by using various symbols, three of social reforms, namely,
eradication of sati-pratha, pardah and imparting to women folk right to preach.

Guru Amardas, the third of the Sikh Gurus, too, was routed to Sikhism by Guru Nanak himself, though he had not the privilege of ever seeing him. Bibi Amro, the daughter of Guru Angad, was married to his nephew. One morning at dawn she was humming some melody. The Vaishnava Amardas yearning for quite sometime to seek some spiritual master who would show him the path leading to salvation heard the melody spell bound. Its magic worked on him. For a moment he felt he had been transported to a world different from his own. From Bibi Amro he knew that the hymn she was humming was a part of Guru Nanak's *Bani*, which he had entrusted to Guru Angad alongwith his entire legacy before his *Nirvana*. He instantly decided to meet Guru Angad.

Guru Amardas was born in 1469 at Basarke in Amritsar to Tej Bhan. He himself the father of four children, two sons Mohri and Mohan and two daughters Dani and Bhani born by Mansa Devi, drawn by the divine glow that he perceived on the face of Guru Angad, bowed at his feet, as soon as he saw him, though Guru Angad was some twenty five years younger to him. Guru Amardas who later came to be known as the ideal of *Guru-sewa* in Sikh-*Panth* dedicated himself with all his faculties and each of his breath to the service of his Guru. Despite his old age and usual rough unfavourable weather in its ever changing moods Guru Amardas walked a distance of over four miles everyday for twelve years to fetch water from the river Beas for his Guru's ablution. It was for such dedication that, when 73, he was nominated by Guru Angad his successor.

Guru Amardas blended with meditation and *Nam-simran* some element of utility. At Goindwal he built a *baoli*, a reservoir, containing 84 steps leading down to the water below. The number of steps was highly symbolic. In Indian thought self was believed to transmigrate through 84 crore births and re-births unless its holy deeds brought it *moksha*. Guru Amardas commanded that commemoration of the *Japuji* on each of the 84 steps of the *baoli* would set the self free from the cycle of these 84 crore births and re-births. Besides its utility, the status of the *baoli* was elevated to that of a shrine, an important step in the religious architecture of the Sikhs.

By decentralizing Guru's power to address congregations through representatives Guru Amardas further widened the *sangat* concept. He set up twenty-two *manjis*, Guru's sub-seats, where his representatives sat to address the local community of Sikhs, who were called *Sangatias*.

Pangat in *langar* concept was now emphasized more than ever before. Community feasting was now as much, or perhaps more, important than the prior community kitchen.

Guru Amardas considered *langar* to have greater sanctity when Guru's *parsad* was taken in *pangat*, that was, when it was taken in community form sitting on ground in disciplined rows. He prescibed "*pahale pangat, pichhe sangat*" and gave *pangat* priority over *sangat*. It is said Mughal emperor Akbar once, when on his way to Lahore, halted at Guru's place to pay him homage. Honouring the tradition Guru Amardas had laid for his disciples Akbar met the Guru only after he took Guru's *parsad* sitting on floor in *pangat* like all others.

Langar in *pangat*, and *pangat* to essentially precede *sangat*, was Guru Amardas' step towards martialization of Sikh community. Guru Amardas had foreseen Mughals' expansionistic designs and his Sikhs likely confrontation with Islamic forces in future. It seems he aimed at building his Sikhs into a community, which could protect itself and its path and pursue it uninterrupted braving whatever came in their way. He wanted to breed amongst his Sikhs a kind of preparedness to face any kind of eventuality. Now man's material form, the mechanism that

produced all thought, had been given as much sanctity as thought itself. With Guru Amardas the prior two-tier Sikh life had assumed the multiplicity of three tiers, that was, they were householders, seekers of truth, and prospective warriors to protect their *Panth* in eventualities.

The credit of conceiving social reforms as an aspect of Sikhism, which gives it today its global form and expansion, too, goes to Guru Amardas. As a social reformer he worked in three directions, eradication of social evils, encouragement of things which could breed a better and stronger society, and creation of new traditions which would encompass within the fold of good-doing and truth-seeking a larger community of man. Eradication of *sati-pratha*, a widow setting herself afire entering her husband's pyre, discouraging *pardah* which widely rendered women-folk incapable to accomplish things which as saints' or soldiers' wives, daughters, or sisters they could be required to do, encouraging inter-caste, inter-creed alliances and widows' re-marriages were some of the far-reaching reforms of Guru Amardas. It was him who introduced women-folk into ecclesiastic body of Sikhism by appointing them to undertake preaching work as *peerahs*.

Guru Amardas considered peace, harmony and conciliation as man's supreme attributes. Revenge had no place in his diction. He considered forgiveness a more potent weapon and believed that patience bred penance in wrong-doer and further that mercy was the greatest of all virtues. His poetry, known as *Anand-geet*, the songs of blissful joy, of which 907 verses are included in the *Adi-granth*, brims with these great ideals and his deep spiritual experiences. Composed in simple lucid style and language his poetry constitutes common man's songs of life. His *Anand Sahib* containing 40 stanzas is sung till date during marriages and on occasions of rejoicing. *Baisakhi* and *Diwali* were his two chosen days in the year when he held a general gathering type congregations for his followers and their families, a tradition which Sikhs follow in some form or the other even today.

Before he abandoned his mortal coil on September 1, 1574 at the age of 95 he nominated his own son-in-law Bhai Jetha to succeed him as Guru Ramdas, the 4th Guru of the Sikhs. Though Bhai Jetha was chosen for his exemplary devotion and exceptional commitment to Sikh tradition, yet Guru Amardas had apparently departed from the prior tradition and had selected for Guruship someone falling in his own family line.

GURU AMARDAS
Sikh, Punjab, Modern, Oil on canvas, Artist: Devender Singh, 1978
Collection: Central Sikh Museum, Amritsar.
Guru Amardas depicted with the pot is both a reality and a symbolism.
He is known to have been fetching water from river Beas for ablution
of his Guru for twelve years. But in Indian tradition ghat or the pot symbolises
the earth and ocean combined, that is the entire cosmos,
which carried, suggest that he mobilised the entire cosmos.

28

Guru Ramdas

Ramdas sarovar nate utre sab paap kamaate

GURU RAMDAS
Guler, Pahari, circa A.D. 1800
Paper, 26 x 22 cm, Acc. no: F-42
Collection: Govt. Museum and Art Gallery, Chandigarh.

Guru Ramdas, born on September 24, 1534 as Jetha in Sodhi Khatri family of Lahore, was married to Bibi Bhani, the daughter of Guru Amardas who was greatly impressed with Jetha's personality and gave him his daughter in marriage. He worked for strengthening the tenets of earlier Gurus but widened and intensified two of the avenues, which Guru Amardas had opened. He had initiated Sikhs' shrines and holy architecture with the construction of great Goindwal *baoli*, where Guru Ramdas, then Jetha, had first met him. Inspired by the construction of the great *baoli* Guru Ramdas founded a city with a tank and another tank Santokhsar. The city founded by him was initially named Ramdaspur to be renamed later as Amritsar and acquire the status of Sikhs' spiritual capital.

For carrying to larger masses the message of Guru Nanak and *Panth* Guru Amardas had initiated the establishment of *manjis,* where the representatives of Guru, usually elderly local Sikhs, preached without a formal appointment. They had a limited role restricted to mere recitation of *Gurbani* and its annotation. Guru Ramdas formalised the representative system. His representatives known as *masand* had powers also for raising funds in Guru's behalf. Such funds Guru Ramdas needed

for the construction of the city and tanks. His *masands* travelled far and wide for fund raising. The concept of elderly local Sikh was largely changed as *masands* were usually outsiders touring with Guru's authority. With this system of *masands* Sikh-*Panth* began acquiring its formal body, which helped consolidate Sikh faith and knit together believers of the faith, scattered far and wide, though later the system also bred corruption.

By constructing a Sikh township Guru Ramdas gave to Sikhs their spiritual capital and a geographical identity. It marked that the Sikh faith had firmly set its foot on the land of Punjab. Constructing a tank with town was not a casual thing. It involved deep symbolism. The tank of Guru Ramdas manifested Punjab, for nothing but waters better symbolised Punjab's land, a creation of waters of five rivers and named after them. A tank created with Sikhs' spiritual geography suggested that the soil of Punjab had Sikhism interwoven with its texture. Besides its utility for bath and consumption a water reservoir, or some other source, built with a Sikh shrine re-creates the symbolism which relate Sikhism and Punjab.

Sikhism was now a regular establishment with its own financial cushion. Besides his efforts to weld Sikhs into a self-conscious and coherent community Guru Ramdas sought to also consoli-

date it financially and structurally. His new township Ramdaspur was not a mere assemblage of brick structures but efforts were made to bring merchants and artisans from other parts to settle and trade there. He commanded his disciples to serve their fellow human beings and eliminate all inequalities. He, thus, aimed at building a financially viable and socially amicable community of his Sikhs.

Guru Ramdas too was a poet of great merit. 638 of his hymns composed in thirty different *ragas* have been included in Sri Guru Granth Sahib. His poetry reveals the intensity of emotions and superb beauty of rhythm. His composition known as *Lavan*, comprising of four line stanzas and used as wedding hymn sung yet on the occasion of Sikh-marriages, is his best known work.

Guru Ramdas, by appointing his younger son Arjan to succeed him as 5th Guru, completely changed the character of Guruship. He was a step ahead to Guru Amardas and paved the way for the concept of family succession of Guruship. Sikhs' political power was now in greater focus as Guru's heir apparent could be better trained for multifarious activities, war eventualities and martial assignments rather than humble *Guru sewa* and spiritualism alone. It had become apparent that Gurus were now born not made.

Guru Arjan

Amrit bani Guru ki mithi, gurmukh wirale kene chakh deethe

GURU ARJAN
Guler, Pahari, circa A.D. 1800
Paper, 26 x 22 cm, Acc. no: F-43
Collection: Lahore Museum, Lahore, Pakistan.

SRI GURU GRANTH SAHIB CARRIED IN A PROCESSION *(Close-up)*
Sikh, Patiala, mid 19th century
Paper, 70 x 89 cm, Acc. no: P/253
Collection: Sheesh Mahal Museum, Patiala.

ਭਾਈਮੀਆਂਸਾਹਿਬਜੀ

Architecture, city planning and creation of new townships, and collection, preservation and standardization of Gurus' *Banis*, the former ones giving to Sikhism its body and geography and the latter ones its mind and soul, were Guru Arjan's priorities. In view of threats, most of which his own ambitious elder brother Prithi Chand, out of frustration and disappointment, mastered, Guru Arjan sought fortification of and scrutinised access to Guru's seat, which changed the face of Sikh Guruship from earlier *Sufiana* bardic sainthood to that of a royal saint with regalia around; from a spiritual empire the Sikhism had come to be a sort of spiritual imperialism where spiritualism was yet its soul and essence but its outer frame had begun to acquire a regal face.

Born on 15th April, 1563 at Goindwal, Arjan was his grandfather Guru Amardas' chosen kinsman to succeed Sikhs' *Guru-gaddi* as fifth Guru of the *Panth*, though he was the youngest son of his father Guru Ramdas. The eighty year grand oldman Guru Amardas had seen on the face of his grandson the celestial glow which, he knew, led anyone born to rarer heights of spiritualism. Guru Amardas not only prophesied that this grandson of his would spread Guru's message across oceans—

*Yeh mera dohita
bani ka bohita benega*

MIAN MIR AND MULLA SHAH WITH DEVOTEES
Sikh–Pahari mix style, early 19th century
Paper, 22.5 x 16.5 cm, Acc. no: D/44
Collection: Sheesh Mahal Museum, Patiala.
*Mian Mir, the Sufi saint who on an invitation from Guru Arjan,
laid the foundation of the Hari Mandir at Amritsar,
something which affirmed the secular tradition of the Sikh Panth.*

From a Sketch by W. Carpenter Jun.ᵣ   J.C. Armytage.

He also took him in his special care with the result that Arjan, when yet quite young, acquired, besides his knowledge in philosophy, language and poetry, exceptional proficiency in music, equestrian sports and archery.

His father's confidence in Guru Arjan was no less. Once when he was otherwise busy, he preferred Arjan to represent him in a marriage at Lahore. Arjan was instructed to return only when he was asked to come back. It was a sort of forced detachment aimed at preparing him to find his own way away from the protective umbrella of his father. At Lahore the young Arjan held congregations, preached Sikhs, held daily communes, and met the known saints, *faqirs* and theologists of his time including the famous *Sufi* saint Mian Mir, Shah Hussain, Chhajju, Mulla Shah, Mukhi Shah and Piloo. His father Guru Ramdas had news of his son's brilliant achievements, he hence did not think of calling him back, though the young Arjan often longed to

be with his reverend father and the Guru. He wrote to him twice but his letters, intercepted by his elder brother Prithi who feared his father might choose Arjan instead of him to succeed him, never reached Guru Ramdas. Finally he wrote him a most pathetic letter in poetry. This letter reached the hands of Guru Ramdas who, highly moved by his son's pathetic yearnings and emotional appeal, instantly sent for him. This letter was a great piece of emotional literature full of pathos:

"My heart longs to have the
sight of the Guru,
In tears it wails like a
chatak bird,
My thirst goeth not,
nor peace I find, without the
sight of the beloved saint,
Sacrifice, O sacrifice, am I unto
the sight of the saint,
my Guru, my beloved,
Pleasing is thy face,
O holy one;
Thy words ringeth one

into the great peace,
How long, how long,
is my separation from the Lord
of the earth to be?
Blessed is the land where thou
livest, O my friend and master,
Sacrifice, O sacrifice am I unto
the Guru, my friend and
beloved and Lord."

It seemed Guru Ramdas awaited his son's return. As soon as he was back, Guru Ramdas entrusted to him *Guru-gaddi*, on September 5, 1581 just four days after he abandoned his mortal frame and merged with the Supreme.

Disappointed and frustrated Prithi, Guru Arjan Dev's elder brother, began creating problems for him. He allied with Mughals just to oust him. Guru Arjan however chose not to pay heed to it and began accomplishing things, which his father had left incomplete. First he took up the construction of the tank at Ramdaspur, renamed later as Amritsar, after this very tank, be-

A *GRANTHI*
Sikh, Punjab, A.D. 1859-62
Artist: William Simpson, Lithograph, 34.5 x 24.4 cm
Collection: Hotel Imperial, New Delhi.
*Granthi was the earliest ecclesiastic position instituted in Sikh tradition right after the installation of
the Adi-granth in Hari Mandir by Guru Arjan. Here the portrayal of the Granthi is most forceful and the
background gives the look of an old gurudwara to suggest perhaps the historicity of granthiship.*

lieved to contain *amrit*, the nectar, the life giving waters of Punjab's five rivers. It needed huge funds. He, hence, began *Guru-gaddi's daswansha seva*, one-tenth of each Sikh's income, a contribution to *Guru-gaddi*. *Masands*, the voluntary workers, were authorised to collect and present to the Guru the *tithe* twice a year on *Baisakhi* and *Diwali*.

He constructed Santokhsar in 1588 and deepened and widened Amritsar tank in 1589. In its centre he constructed Sikhs' holiest shrine, Hari Mandir. Its foundation was laid by the famous *Sufi* saint Mian Mir, which defined the secular character of Sikhism. It had openings on all four sides to let all directions merge into it and to symbolise its universality. He often acclaimed that Nanak's path was for all, whatever their caste or creed, or the direction they came from or bowed to. Guru Arjan founded Tarantaran and Kartarpur and on the river Beas Sri Hargobindpur. Tarantaran had

a huge tank, large *dharamsala* and a leprosarium.

In Sikh tradition, music and poetry were used for enlivening *sangat*, conveying thought and realising the Supreme. *Langar*, or the later *pangat*, the instruments of equality and disciplined community life, too, were its initial organs. With the establishment of *manjis* began decentralization of Guruship and with appointed ones preaching in Guru's behalf the expansion of his spiritual powers. The *baoli* at Goindwal marked the beginning of Sikh architecture and towns and tanks their efforts to seek their geographical identity and create own spiritual geography. Reforms and eradication of social evils began simultaneously.

Guru Arjan devoted himself to strengthening this basic Sikh tradition. He identified its four avenues to sustain and strengthen, *Gurus' bani*, overall management of Sikh affairs, Sikhs' sectarian architecture, and service of mankind helping

needy, effecting various reforms and combating social wrongs and evils. With the construction of Hari Mandir and Gurdwaras in other towns, and by giving them a definite architectural form, which combined military fortification with congregational provisions to cover eventualities, Guru Arjan gave to Sikhism its own architecture. He infused with Gurdwara architecture aesthetics, engraving, carving and murals. This form of Sikh shrines as evolved now, a contribution of Guru Arjan, sustains yet, in spirit and form, almost unchanged.

Guru Arjan's tanks, besides their symbolism, and *dharamsala* were amenities to serve the needy. A plan of leprosarium in Tarantaran reflected his deep feeling and concern for suffering humanity giving to Sikhism such ideals of service that a Sikh would even stake his life in realising them. It was in pursuance to this traditon of service that the child Guru Har Kishan, when only eight years, lost his life in helping the

GURU ARJAN SERVING LEPERS AT TARAN-TARAN
Sikh, Modern
Oil on canvas, 35.5" x 29"
Artist: Devender Singh, 1978
Collection: Punjab and Sind Bank, New Delhi.
Taran-Taran by its very name suggests redemption from miseries of life.
By creating a centre for serving lepers there, Guru Arjan gave Taran-Taran an added meaning.

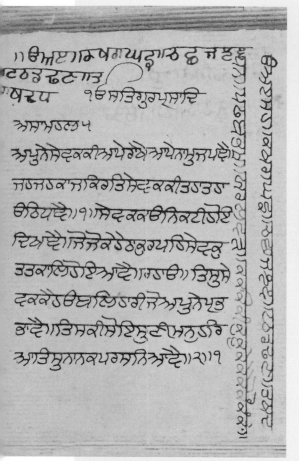

victims of small pox at Delhi, when during his visit the epidemic broke out there.

Guru Arjan gave to Sikh affairs a definite shape. *Guru-gaddi* or *manjis* were no more abstract things. Gurdwaras' material form transformed the *Guru-gaddi* from an abstract concept to a materially present entity, though its basic spiritual context and ultimate manifestation in Guru himself, was yet the same. *Masands*, the erstwhile casual representatives, worked now under formal authority and appointment. *Panth's* finances were better managed under a rational system. *Guru-gaddi's* share was defined as *dasmansha*, the one-tenth of a Sikh's earning and *Masands*, were the official agency to collect it. The congregations held on *Baisakhi* and *Diwali* were regular, better organised and also purposive for *masands* were required to essentially attend them and deposit the *dasmansha* they had collected in between.

Guru Arjan's most invaluable contribution was compilation of the sacred *Adi-granth*, aimed at preserving and perpetuating *Gurbani*. The *Adi-granth* consisted of the poetry of the first four Gurus, hymns of Vaishnava and *Sufi* saints and the ethical, moral and devotional poetry of Hindu and Muslim poets which the first four Gurus had adopted as part of *Panth's bani* considering it as much and as adequately conveying the pith of their teachings. The *Adi-granth* first time shaped the canons of Sikh philosophy and thought, or rather the totality of Sikhism, a seed sprouting later into a well pruned tree with its own shape and shade. It manifested a systematic effort at closely exploring and weaving together music, faith and thought, the senses, the heart and the mind, combining into one single whole all faculties of the devotional being seeking the truth of life and universe, which is the essence of Sikhism.

In conveying the *Gurbani* from devotees' alcoves and singers' throats to the sacred *vedika* of the newly constructed Hari Mandir, Guru Arjan had many hurdles. Besides scriptural incorrectness, superimpositions and omissions and ill suiting musical modes, those who possessed holy *pothis*, the scanty collections of *Gurus'bani*, were unwilling to part with them. Emissaries were always on toes to rush wherever a line or leaf was known to exist. However, it had its own problems.

A LEAF WITH *PENTI-AKHARI*
"the thirty five syllables of Gurmukhi" in Guru Arjan's handwriting
Collection: Bhai Suchet Singh, village Bhai Rupa, Moga, Punjab.
*The family claims that this leaf containing 35 syllables of Gurmukhi script is
in the hand writing of Guru Arjan and is one of the several relics which
Guru Hargobind had entrusted to his close disciple and
Bhai Suchet Singh's ascendant Bhai Rupa who later founded this village.*

For collecting the sacred *Pothis* from Baba Mohanji, the eldest son of Guru Amardas, Guru Arjan had to go personally. When Baba Mohanji refused to see Bhai Gurdas and the oldest Sikh Baba Buddaji, baptised by Guru Nanak himself, went to him for acquiring the holy *pothis*, Guru Arjan himself traveled to Goindwal and reached his house. Collecting his entire spiritual strength and blending it into his voice Guru Arjan began singing on Baba Mohanji's door a hymn, immortalising it, in praise of Mohan, Mohan the Lord, and Baba Mohan, who held the great legacy of Gurus. He sang:

> *O Mohan,*
> *Thou abidest in a heavenly*
> *home of infinite glory,*
> *Thy abode is beauteous, the*
> *sanctuary of saints,*
> *Yea, of infinite glory is thy*
> *sanctuary,*
> *O Thou beneficent Master, and*
> *all sing Thy praise,*
> *And, wherever gather the*
> *saints, they dwell on thee,*
> *Take pity on the meek, O Thou*
> *beneficent One,*
> *Nanak prays Thee,*
> *I seek to see Thy sight*
> *Whereby I attain to the peace*
> *of piety.*

Melted with Guru Arjan's celestial melody Baba Mohanji emerged from his house, preserved till date as *Chaubara Baba Mohanji*, a *tirtha* for Sikhs, and presented to Guru Arjan the holy *pothis*. The *pothis* were carried to Amritsar in a palanquin in full ceremony, hundreds of Sikhs moving in procession with Guru Arjan himself walking bare-footed behind. The result of such efforts, correction of material so piled and its compilation was the holy *Adi-granth*. The Holy Book was then installed in Hari Mandir with full rituals and was revered by Guru Arjan Dev himself as the light of the Gurus and, hence, an entity of a status greater and higher than that of any living one and himself. The later Sikh cult of revering the holy *Granth* as Guru obviously had its roots in the deity like installation of the *Adi-granth* and a living Guru's, that is, Guru Arjan's reverence for it.

Guru Arjan Dev's life gave to Sikhism a lot, but no less gave his death, a sacrifice he made for his adherence to the *Panth* laying the tradition of sacrifice in Sikhism. A true saint had no other option but to bless him who came to his threshold. As a Sikh Guru, Guru Arjan had also to feed whoever reached his *langar*. Mughal emperor Jahangir's son Khusraw, turned a rebel against his own father within a few months of his father's succession, when on his way to Lahore, happened to pass across Guru Arjan Dev's *dwar* and seek the Saint's blessings. Khusraw was blessed and his soldiers, whatever their number, served food at *langar*. Guru Arjan Dev, a saint, had blessed a man's goodness, not the rebellion in him, and had fed the hunger, not the revenge in anyone's blood. Mughal emperor Jahangir, however, failed to appreciate a saint's way and got Guru Arjan Dev arrested and put to severe torture and humiliation, which ultimately deprived him of his life. Deeply

aggrieved and bitterly humiliated community of Sikhs felt the sainthood would always be in peril unless protected by strong arms. The martyrdom of Guru Arjan Dev by itself could have instrumented an upheaval in the history of Sikhs. But his last message to his son and successor, Hargobind, "let him sit fully armed on the throne and maintain an army to the best of his ability", brought a tremendously positive change in Sikhism. The sainthood was yet the same in its spirit and object but its outer frame was fortified to face eventualities.

BHAI GURDAS (1543-1637)
Sikh, Modern, Oil on canvas
Artist: Gurdit Singh, 1975
Collection: Punjab and Sind Bank, New Delhi.
Bhai Gurdas assisted Guru Arjan in compilation of Adi-Granth,
however his own poetry was not included in the Adi-Granth, though,
it was given the status of the key to the holy Granth by Guru Arjan.

Guru Hargobind

Gobind guni nidhan gurmukh janiye, hoi kirpal dayal har rang maniye

GURU HARGOBIND IN HIS *DARBAR*
Sikh–Pahari mix style, mid 19th century
Paper, Acc. no: D/37
Collection: Sheesh Mahal Museum, Patiala

uru Hargobind who combined in his personality a saint, a sportsman, a soldier, and a national military hero of the people of Punjab, and the only such one in six hundred years after its conquest by Muslims, succeeded to the *Guru-gaddi* and commanded Sikhs only when eleven. His father's sufferings and sacrifice had only hardened him and he was better prepared and more determined to face any sufferings and make any sacrifice and thus aptly follow his father and carry out his mission.

Guru Hargobind, born on June 14, 1595 at Wadali, some eight kilometers west of Amritsar, came out with a different vision of Guruship. To him it represented both the *Miri* and *Piri*, *Shakti* and *Bhakti*, or *Tegh* and *Degh*, that was, the soldier and the saint. He used to tie two swords instead of usual one, one each on right and left, to symbolise a Sikh Guru's two roles. It is said Baba Buddaji, one of the two chosen Sikhs of Guru Nanak, while

(Left) GANGA SAGAR OF GURU HARGOBIND
Collection: Bhai Rattan Singh of Daroli Bhai, Moga, Punjab.

(Above) DAGGER OR *KATAR*
Sikh, Punjab, early 19th century
Steel with gold work, 43 x 10 cm, Acc. no: 74/13
Collection: Qila Mubarak, Patiala.
The hilt is inscribed in Gurmukhi characters, most probably the Japuji Sahib.
Though partially damaged, it reveals the fine quality of calligraphy.
The blade is double edged and highly tempered to remain yet Abdar.

dane things spiritual sanctity and hue and made it a part of Sikhism, a part of the service rendered to the Supreme. Guru Hargobind built in Amritsar a fortress, though a small one and hence insignificant defence-wise, yet in the growth of Sikh architecture, it was a mile stone. It marked Sikhs' architectural journey seeking new dimensions from Guru's humble *dwar*, the Gurdwara, to sainthood's fortified abode, robust and mighty, guarded by Sikhs' potent swords. Another massive structure, a building known as *Akal-Takht*, to remain known as such ever after, constructed facing Hari Mandir, added yet new dimensions to Sikhism. It was Guru Hargobind's supreme seat, and again to remain as such ever after, for discussing defence, military plans, conquests and other political matters, for imparting justice and for holding congregations, other than religious or devotional, where bards and poets recited annals, lores and ballads extolling feats of heroism and great chivalry. This brought secular heroic poetry and non-religious type literature into Sikh tradition widening its creative and imaginative periphery. Guru Hargobind created, thus, a kind of Sikh sovereignty, where Sikhs had their own governance, own entity, own law and a forum of their own to settle issues.

coronating Guru Hargobind, the fifth Guru to be coronated by him, erroneously tied the sword on Guru Hargobind's left. Realising the error Baba Buddaji sought to re-tie it on his right, but Guru Hargobind asked Baba Buddaji to tie one more on his right and announced that he would carry two swords, instead of one, the one to chastise the oppressor and the other to protect the innocent. He is said to declare that Guru's house would henceforth combine spiritual and mundane powers, the rosary would be his sword-belt and an emblem of royalty would crown his turban. The Sikhs were instructed to keep a horse and carry a sword. The aureole of Guru Nanak's Sikhism and the humming melodies of his *sangats* had now combined with them the dazzling brilliance and the deafening sound of swords.

The Sikhs were trained in the art of sword-handling, fighting and hunting, and Guru Hargobind spent everyday some time in training a group of Sikhs and in hunting and games. It imparted to such military acts and mun-

GURU HARGOBIND ON HIS BLACK STALLION
Sikh, Punjab, Paper, mid 19th century
Collection: S.S. Hitkari, New Delhi
The presence of hawk and dog suggests that Guruji is on a hunting errand which had
become by his days an essential part of chivalry. Under the concept of Piri and Miri
Guru Hargobind was commanded to manage the Panth like a warrior.

However, before Sikh resistance was formidable, Guru Hargobind was imprisoned by Mughals apparently under the pretext of his failure to pay the fine imposed on his father but the ulterior reasons for his arrest too were as much obvious. His recourse to arms, fortification and militarization was not palatable to the Mughal power. Later however, the known *Sufi* saint Mian Mir intervened and convinced the Mughal emperor Jahangir to release Guru Hargobind. In Gwalior fort, where he had been imprisoned, he was revered by other alike imprisoned rulers as their spiritual guardian. They called him *'Baba'*. Guru Hargobind here too had a saint's role. He decided not to move out unless his fellow prisoners too were set free. Out of gratitude and love they called him now *'Baba Bandi Chhor'* or *'Data Bandi Chhor'*. The essence of Guru Hargobind's being was sainthood, in prison, battlefield or beyond, the very marrow of Sikh tradition.

Despite Mughal pressure and Shahjahan's orthodox and hostile policy towards Guru Hargobind he resumed his plans of militarizing his Sikhs and strengthening his concept of *Miri* and *Piri* soon after he was set free. *'Sachcha Patshah'* was now the title, he was addressed with, by his loving and devoted Sikhs. It is said Chhatrapati Shivaji's Guru Swami Ramdas once questioned

his sainthood in context to his bearing a sword, riding a horse and calling himself *'Sachcha Patshah'*. Guru Hargobind is said to have replied, *'Batan faqiri, zahir amiri'*, that was, 'saintliness was within, sovereignty was without'. Later Swami Ramdas prepared Shivaji to be saint within and soldier without.

Guru Hargobind fought against Mughals six times, though in view of Mughals' huge military power he had to shift his headquarters first from Amritsar to Sri Har Gobindpur, then to Kartarpur,

and finally to Kiratpur close to the borders of Kahlur now in Himachal. During the last decade of his life, he was at Kiratpur devoted to *Panth's* propagation and Almighty's service. In his effort to give his Sikhs an emblem of regality and an identity of their own, Guru Hargobind devised for his troops a pennant to become thenafter the flag of Sikhism now known as the *Nishan Sahib* and kettledrums, though for a distinct identity of their own, Sikhs had to wait for some seventy years more till the birth of *Khalsa*.

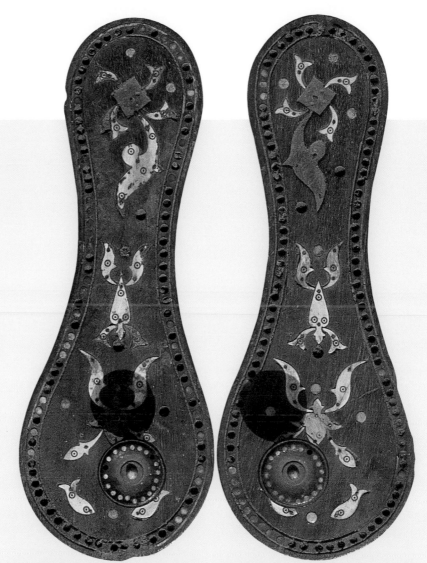

PADUKAS OF GURU HARGOBIND
from a private collection
*In Indian tradition of faith padukas has for a devotee same significance
as a shrine. By touching paduka a devotee not only felt the touch of
his master but also expressed the extremity of his humbleness.*

Guru Har Rai

Amrit bani har har teri, sun sun hove param gat meri

GURU HAR RAI
Guler, Pahari, circa A.D. 1800
Paper, 16 x 22 cm, Acc. no: F-45
Collection: Govt. Museum and Art Gallery, Chandigarh

Guru Hargobind's fourteen-year old grandson Har Rai, born on 30th January, 1630 A.D. at Kiratpur, succeeded his grandfather Guru Hargobind to *Guru-gaddi* after he passed away in 1644. Neither of his two sons, Surajmal and Tegh Bahadur, was willing to take up the responsibility of leading and guiding the community of Sikhs. Tegh Bahadur, though a recluse when his father Guru Hargobind died, later took to Sikhism and was nominated Sikhs' Nineth Guru.

Guru Har Rai continued the cult of *Miri* and *Piri* and maintained a splendid court and a company of 200 mounted soldiers as his personal guard, yet he felt the proportion of *Miri* in Sikhism was gradually mounting with a result that in the life of an average Sikh the 'spiritual' was seen usually subserving the 'material'. He did not, hence, have much preference for warfare and chose rather the solitude of hills where, while meditating within, he was able to explore and collect his energies for applying them to consolidate the spiritual part of Sikhism. He believed that in Sikh tradition warfare was an eventuality and spiritualism its essence.

He sought to revive Guru Nanak's way though his canvas was not that wide. He believed like the first Guru that personal touch and contact was the most effective instrument for inspiring the Sikhs. He, hence, undertook tours, though only of shorter durations and distances, which, perhaps, the later sovereign form of Sikh Guruship conditioned. He stayed at Nahan, now in Himachal, for some twelve years and wielded great spiritual influence around. He visited Nathana many times. He once blessed there a Jat boy, poor and hungry, who later came to found the known *Phulkian* family after his own name *Phul*. This family later ruled the states of Patiala, Nabha, and Jind. A *bairagi* monk Bhagat Gir met here Guru Har Rai and was so impressed that he took to Sikhism. Renamed as Bhagat Bhagwan he was commissioned to carry to the eastern part Guru Nanak's message. Wherever Guru Har Rai went hundreds of people heard him and got converted to Sikhism. At Kiratpur, Bhai Sangatia, a man of great calibre came in his touch. He not only joined Sikhism but also undertook the mission of spreading the message of Guru Nanak in *Bari Doab*. His other associate Bhai Gonda carried the mission to Lahore and converted their people to Nanak's path.

Sainthood with no place for vengeance and ill-will was the legacy of Guru Har Rai too. He had

GURU HAR RAI WITH HIS GRANDFATHER GURU HARGOBIND
Sikh, Punjab, Modern, Oil on canvas
Artist: Bodh Raj, 1990
Collection: Punjab and Sind Bank, New Delhi.
After the Guruship had come to be a matter of dynastic descendance the would be Gurus were accordingly prepared for the responsibilities. Here in the painting Guru Hargobind seems to be guiding his grandson Har Rai as to matters of guruship.

in his possession a life saving medicine, which the Mughal emperor Shahjahan needed for saving the life of his eldest and the most beloved son Dara Shikoh who was struggling in between life and death. Shahjahan's messenger, sent to Guru Har Rai, went back not with the medicine alone but also with his holy blessings to emperor's ailing son. Dara Shikoh speedily recovered but whether by Guru's medicine or his blessing was not known. Guru Har Rai only strengthened the tradition of Sikh Gurus which believed in returning good for evil.

Despite his aversion for warfare and violence, he would not hesitate to confront with any power or pay whatever cost for his adherence to truth and his *Panth*. Misled to believe that Guru Har Rai was a rebel, and that Sikh scriptures propagated things against Islam, the Mughal emperor Aurangzeb, after he had succeeded his father, summoned Guru Har Rai to his court, though the letter he sent to him was very polite, something such as a dagger wrapped in velvet. Guru Har Rai nominated his eldest son Ram Rai to visit the Mughal emperor. He was instructed not to appease the Mughal emperor by his words, perform miracles or to interpret *Adi-granth*, or any of its parts, to mean different from what it actually meant. Charmed by Mughal power and the glamour of the Mughal court Ram Rai

acted differently. He appeased the emperor and disobeyed his father. He performed miracles and interpreted Adi Granth to emperor's liking. After Guru Har Rai had heard all about it he reacted that "Guruship was tigress' milk and could not be contained in a pot other than that of gold". He announced that Ram Rai would never appear before him. He disowned him and nominated his second son Har Kishan, though just five, as his successor.

Guru Har Rai often recited:

" *Hearts are jewels,*
Distress them not,
Those who distress no heart
seek the beloved God,"

a couplet of Baba Farid, which suggested that the great Sikh Guru considered compassion as the highest virtue of all things divine in man. Whether real or imagined, an incident of his life has been widely covered in Sikh literature and in medieval Sikh paintings. While strolling in a garden he dragged with his loose cloak a few stem-containing flowers. No sooner he saw the flowers falling to ground his eyes welled with tears. It pained him that he instrumented them injury, an act which was never in his nature. In Guru Har Rai Sikhism seemed to seek the apex of emotionality and the softer aspects of human life.

PORTRAIT OF GURU HAR RAI
From Persian manuscript of the *Military Manual* of Maharaja Ranjit Singh.
Sikh, Punjab, circa A.D. 1830-40
Paper, 28.5 x 19 cm, Acc. no: 1035/3
Collection: Maharaja Ranjit Singh Museum, Amritsar.

Guru Har Kishan

Guru Har Kishan dhyayiye, Jis dhithe sab dukh jaye

MIRZA RAJA ZAI SINGH PAYING HOMAGE TO CHILD–SAINT GURU HAR KISHAN
Late Mughal, circa A.D. 1740-50
Paper, 22 x 17 cm, Acc. no: 61.831
Collection: National Museum, New Delhi.

Guru Har Kishan, born of Guru Har Rai and Mata Sulakkhani, succeeded to *Guru-gaddi* only when five years of age. He was exceptionally intelligent and wise for his age. He was able to instruct and guide his Sikhs, resolve their issues and remove their doubts. He had such spiritual strength as could lead his Sikhs to salvation.

He passed away when only eight, yet made his life, and thus Sikhism, the highest ideal of service of sufferers, the seed of which Guru Arjan had laid in constructing leprosarium at Tarantaran consecrating service to mankind as the highest divinity in man. He was summoned by Aurangzeb to examine the complaint his elder brother Ram Rai had lodged with the Mughal emperor. It related to his so-called illegal succession. He was unwilling to go but the intervention of Mirzaraja Jai Singh of Amber prevailed. As the Sikh tradition has it, Guru Har Kishan was received at Mughal court with full honour and stayed where stands today Gurdwara Bangla Sahib.

When yet in Delhi, an epidemic, the small pox, broke out. It was a divine trial of Guru Har Kishan's saintliness. Along with his Sikhs, Guru Har Kishan plunged into the service of suffering mankind, attending many victims personally. In the process he himself fell prey to it. He was under high fever and unconscious for many days. In the morning on March 30, 1664 he opened his eyes to utter Baba Bakala and left the ephemeral world. His last rites were performed on Yamuna's bank, where stands now the Gurdwara Bala Sahib.

With his unflinching courage and commitment to serve suffering humanity, Guru Har Kishan established that his eight years' age was not the age of Sikhism. His courage, humanism, commitment to serve the sufferer and his saintliness were all born of a great tradition to which generations of man, his predecessors, the Gurus, their Sikhs, bards, poets, singers, thinkers, saints, *faqirs, yogis, bairagis*, house-holders and recluse and many more had contributed. Thus the age of virtue, goodness and concern for suffering humanity in his eight-year mortal body was simply immeasurable for time had spanned his mortal frame but not his inherent saintliness, which was neither born of it nor confined to it.

THE BOUNTEOUS GURU HAR KISHAN
Sikh, Punjab, Modern, Oil on canvas
Artist: G.S. Sohan Singh, 1976
Collection: Baba Baghel Singh Museum, Bangla Sahib Gurdwara, New Delhi.
*When Guru Har Kishan was at Delhi on an invitation of Mughal emperor, a huge crowd
of his devotees seeking remedy to their sufferings gathered round the Guru.
The bounteous child Guru Har Kishan blessed all with something or the other.*

Guru Tegh Bahadur

Gun Gobind gayo nahin, janam akarath kin,
Kah Nanak har bhaj mana, jeh bidh jal ko min

GURU TEGH BAHADUR
Guler, Pahari, circa A.D. 1800
Paper, 16 x 22 cm, Acc. no: F-47
Collection: Lahore Museum, Lahore, Pakistan.
Known for his unregistering sacrifice Guru Tegh Bahadur was as great sword player
and warrior. When he was seventeen and bore his birth name Tyagmal was awarded
the title of Tegh Bahadur for his distinctive achievements of his sword. The painter seems to have blended
here with Guru's saintly personality the elements of his youthful days.

uru Tegh Bahadur, one of Guru Har-Gobind's two sons, who had declined *Guru-gaddi* earlier in 1644 when his father passed away, was the Baba Bakala of the semi-conscious eighth Sikh Guru Har Kishan, though it were the believing Sikhs who discovered and compelled him with their love and devotion to accept their leadership. In his father's lifetime Guru Teg Bahadur had turned to asceticism and was a *sanyasi* with his seat at Bakala. He was detached with whatever happened around.

Many hypocrites, after they knew that Guru Har Kishan, before he had closed his eyes, wished some Baba Bakala to take over the *Guru-gaddi*, installed themselves as Sikhs' ninth Guru and established their *gaddis*. It is said Bakala had at one time more than twenty-four self-styled Sikh Gurus all claiming genuineness. There was great confusion and genuine Sikhs looked for the real Master to guide and protect them.

All felt so helpless.

It is said, Makkhan Shah Lubana, a devout Sikh trader of Jammu, had his ship with full cargo caught in a storm. He invoked Guru Nanak for saving it and vowed to contribute five hundred gold coins to the *Panth* in case the ship ported safe. It was saved, but by then Guru Har Kishan had passed away and *Panth* had no nominee. Like others Makkhan Shah too reached Bakala looking for Nanak's nominee. Finding that Bakala had

At Anandpur Sahib the aggrieved Brahmins from Kashmir narrating to
Guru Tegh Bahadur and his son Gobind Rai the atrocities inflicted by Mughals
Sikh, Punjab, Modern, Oil on canvas,
Artist: G.S. Sohan Singh
Collection: Baba Baghel Singh Museum, Bangla Sahib Gurudwara, New Delhi.

instead many Gurus he decided to bow to all but offered to each just two coins. He also heard of a non-Sikh recluse away from town's hubbub. He went to him as well, knelt and offered him his usual two coins. The recluse winked his eyes, blessed the trader and asked why he offered just two whereas he had vowed for five hundred. Tears of joy rolled Makkhan Shah's eyes. He ran to the housetop and cried enrapt, "*Guru laboji Guru laboji*-I have found the Guru, I have found the Guru". But for a few dissenting notes Makkhan Shah's discovery was widely applauded. Multitudes of believers of the *Panth* began thronging Bakala, and compelled by their love and devotion the 'recluse' to carry Guru Nanak's torch and lead and protect his Sikhs.

In an event, when Aurangzeb, the most fanatic staunch Musalman such as history had not known many, was seeking to convert to Islam everyone with a tyrant's hand inflicting death and terrible atrocities, and non-Muslims under threat to life, property, respect and grace were forcibly swept to it, Guru Tegh Bahadur chose to resist against forced conversions and to insist for an individual's right to his religion, something which the Constitution of free sovereign India envisaged as peoples' fundamental right three hundred years later.

Guru Tegh Bahadur was aware of Mughals' invicible might and knew that an armed resistance would least prevail, particularly when Indians, engulfed in fear, had lost confidence in themselves, their values, traditions, creeds and their past. Guru Tegh Bahadur felt his role was wider encompassing all, not mere Sikhs, and his weapon had to be more effective than mere arms for arms only beheaded but neither improved the quality of head nor of heart and hardly ever changed the face of time or universe. He hence aimed somewhat differently and had an unconventional approach.

Freedom of religion, insistence for ethical and moral values, resistance against oppression, forced conversions, and a preparedness for any kind of sacrifice were, thus, the pivotal points of Guru Tegh Bahadur's Sikhism. More than a religious teacher he sought in a Sikh Guru, or in a Sikh, and thus in himself, a social reformer who could revitalise the people's confidence in their own values and creeds, boost their morale, strengthen their commitment to their own ideologies and faith, make them fearless and prepare them for any sacrifice.

Much like Guru Nanak, Guru Tegh Bahadur believed in individual goodness, for individual constituted the basic unit of society or even of world and his goodness the essence of universal goodness. He travelled far and wide for he believed that thus alone he would reach them whose confidence he aimed at reviving. He seemed to have a feeling that Sikh movement had for sometime inclined, or confined, to protect and promote Sikhs, instead of Sikhism. To Guru Tegh Bahadur Sikhism comprised of values which were widely intrinsic and sustained only by inner strength, but Sikh movement had of late inclined to arms and managing exterior. He believed a preparedness for sacrifice alone strengthened the inner for it always insisted for values and desisted fear and compromises. It rekindled total inner being. Sacrifice, though it wasn't new in Sikh tradition, was the core of Guru Teg Bahadur's thought and was somewhat differently conceived. To him sacrifice was the most potent weapon of resistance for he believed that the loss of one life, or of a few, kindled life in millions. His own sacrifice aimed at relieving the oppressed many who out of fear of life had given up what was their best. Sacrifice, as Guru Teg Bahadur conceived, had not to be mere wilful but also the supreme will.

Once a huge crowd of desperate Kashmiri Brahmins, oppressed by Mughal *Subedar* attempting their conversion by sword and massacring the persisting ones, came to him at Anandpur. Guru Teg Bahadur realised that fear for life was these Brahmins' problem for they misconsidered life more precious than life's values. He felt some leading one's sacrifice alone could revive their lost spirits and restore their confidence. His innocent young son Govind Rai, who stood besides him, asked his father what disturbed him so much. He explained to him all and that the sacrifice of someone, such as did not go unnoticed, could relieve them of their plight. He said, he was thinking who would be best suited. Gobind Rai, not knowing its implications, innocently uttered, "who better than him!" The child's utterance kindled in Guru Teg Bahadur the supreme will, the determination to sacrifice. He instructed the crowd to go and tell its Subedar that they would all take to Islam if he converted Guru Teg Bahadur.

The news had reached Aurangzeb who was already unhappy with Sikhs for giving their Guru the title of *Sachcha Patshah*, which derogated the authority of the Mughal emperor suggesting by implication that he was false. He hence wished to eliminate Sikhs completely. Guru Tegh Bahadur was summoned to Mughal court and sentenced to death. On November 11, 1675 he was put to death, but before his beheaded body was exposed to public view Bhai Jetha, one of his devotees, succeeded in transporting his head to Anandpur, now Anandpur Sahib, where his son

Gobind Rai cremated it. The rest of him was cremated at Delhi where now Gurdwara Rakabganj immortalises his memory.

His eleven year tenure as Sikh Guru was remarkable in many things. His travels encompassing Agra, Allahabad, Patna, most parts of Bengal, Assam, Malwa and Punjab were quite extensive and also broad-based. His approach was humanistic. During his tours he built wells, *dharmsalas*, planted trees, distributed cows to poor and acquired land and gave it to landless farmers. When in eastern part he met several scholars, *pirs, faqirs* and *yogis* and other knowledgeable persons. Despite only his humanistic approach thousands of people joined his *Panth* with a result that most of this region was studded with Sikh shrines. When in Assam, he learnt that Aurangzeb wanted to convert *Dar-ul-Harb* into *Dar-ul-Islam* with an aim to eliminate Brahmins completely. Aurangzeb contemplated that this would render Hindu centres of learning rootless and, as such the system would completely collapse. For intensifying his efforts to avert Aurangzeb's designs he came first to Patna and then to Anandpur.

Guru Tegh Bahadur excelled in pathetic poetry. He sang of the sorrows of created life but led them to convert into the vision of heaven. He had a preference for Brijbhasha, easy, smooth, simple, and unembellished. His poetry was

born of his experiences of real life, spiritual discipline of the highest order, his philosophic wisdom and his enlightenment. After the compilation of the *Adi-granth* he was the only Guru to resort to poetry writing. Of his poetry 59 *shabdas* and 57 *slokas* were included in the *Adi-granth* by his son Guru Gobind Singh before it was consecrated as the Sri Guru Granth Sahib.

Guru Tegh Bahadur's mission as a Sikh Guru did not restrict to Sikhs alone. For seeking his benevolence a sufferer was not required to take to Sikhism, especially when he was unconvinced, as this would have derogated his own conviction of religious freedom and protection of the right of everyone to practise his faith freely. Guru Nanak had refused to wear *Janeu*, Hindus' sacred thread, whereas Guru Tegh Bahadur laid his life to protect Hindus' right to wear it with full freedom. He was, perhaps, the only one in the history to have staked his life for other people's faith. In his non-violent resistance, in his insistence for the freedom of religion and reverence for others' faith, in his adherence for human values and moral and ethical norms and in his preparedness to make any sacrifice for any of his adherences, Guru Tegh Bahadur seems to have guided the course of India's Freedom Movement and has as much relevance today.

Guru Gobind Singh

Mein hoon param purukh ka dasa, dekhan ayo jagat tamasha

A SWORD OF TENTH GURU
Circa A.D. 1700, 100 x 11 cm, Acc. no: 59
Collection: Qila Mubarak, Patiala
*The Persian inscription on the sword acclaims its place on the girdle of the Guruji presented
to him by Yar Muhammad of Surat. Guruji later entrusted it to Bhai Dharm Singh at Nanded
when the latter was returning to Bagharian, his native place. The sword later passed on to
Raja Gajpat Singh, the founder of the Jind state. In 1948 this sword and the Katar were
transferred from the state of Jind to the Qila Mubarak, Patiala.*

The quiet unresisting meek sacrifice of Guru Tegh Bahadur, so shocking, painful and unbelievable, and ignominious on the part of the Islamic rulers, precipitated in Sikh life a deep commotion and once again turned the tide of the Sikh movement towards militarization. The might of arms, sectarian unity, community identity and distinction and intrepidity were now again as essential in Sikh life as spiritualism and sainthood. It was widely felt that goodness, virtue, saintliness and all that belonged to spirit within essentially required the mighty cover of without, the community of believers had also to be the community that fought to its goals, the spiritual routed via material.

Gobind Rai, when nine running, ascended the *Guru-gaddi* with his father's, or more so, a saint's head in hand, mutilated brutally and deconsecrated, and with deep turbulence and agony in mind. The boy knew little of his father's concept of non-violent resistance-free sacrifice but a lot of antipathy and cruelty the sainthood had met with, and its testimony he had at hand. He felt that sainthood without strength to protect it was hardly of any avail. A determination, which every inch of space he trod strengthened, crept up into his mind. He decided to brace his material fold first and seek only thenafter the means of spiritual elevation. He was not unacquainted with Sikh tradition embracing both the *Miri* and *Piri* requiring a Sikh to be soldierly and saintly together. He resolved to strengthen this aspect and lead the community to a rationalized modern militia.

Gobind Rai was born at Patna on December 22, 1666 when his father Guru Tegh Bahadur, leaving his mother and his pregnant wife at Patna in the care of local Sikhs, was on his Assam tour. Every moment after his birth was a miracle, and an arduous trial after he assumed *Guruship*. As the tradition has it, when born,

54

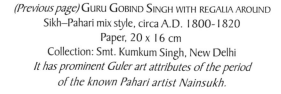
(Previous page) GURU GOBIND SINGH WITH REGALIA AROUND
Sikh–Pahari mix style, circa A.D. 1800-1820
Paper, 20 x 16 cm
Collection: Smt. Kumkum Singh, New Delhi
*It has prominent Guler art attributes of the period
of the known Pahari artist Nainsukh.*

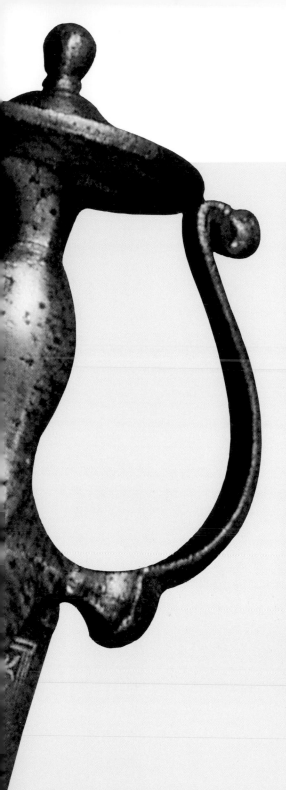

*Guruji's one more sword is in the possession of the
Maharani of erstwhile state of Jaipur.
She had brought it from Sirmur after her marriage with Maharaja Bhavani
Singh of Jaipur. Sirmur, now in H.P. was formerly a part of Punjab
and Sirmur ruling family had great affinity with the Tenth Guru.
This sword is annually displayed for Darshan in Jaipur.*

he was endowed with an exceptional glow and benign celestial look. When hardly six- months, he walked and before a year spoke distinctly well. In his childhood itself he had a leader's qualities commanding his age group in matters of games and sports, and won all hearts, young and old alike, by his handsome and unique personality and great charm of manners. He was excellent in archery or whatever taught. He had princely grace and grew a prince-like from days to weeks and months.

Legends assign his childhood lot of strangeness. With child's mystic indications Muslim saint Bhikam Shah of Gharam was led to pronounce that he would found for both, Hindu and Musalman, the path of righteousness. He had come to see Guru Tegh Bahadur's new born son. When yet at Patna, he intuitively knew Maini Rani's wish and fulfilled it. The childless lady, whenever she saw Gobind Rai pass with his child-army along her house, wished that he walked into her house, called her mother and asked for some *chhole- pooris* for himself and his army. In the gust of such impulse she one day actually cooked some *chhole-pooris*, and began awaiting him, and to her utter dismay and the greatest ever delight a little after she found Gobind Rai with his army standing before her.

No less strange was the incident at Danapur, the village he passed across on his way to Anandpur Sahib. Hurt and slighted by *masands* by refusing to accept her meagre contribution the poor old mother Jamuna was long awaiting the Guru himself to come and accept her hotch-potch, which out of a frenzy she prepared everyday and waited for the Guru. And, the old grandma, confident as she was that he would sure come a day, was least surprised when she saw Gobind Rai standing before her and asking for his hotch-potch, which she had prepared for him.

In February 1672, when a little more than five, he reached Anandpur Sahib. Appropriate

55

arrangements were instantly made for teaching him Gurmukhi, Persian, Sanskrit and Hindi and for training him in sword handling, riding, hunting, swimming and archery. He also acquired great proficiency in techniques of warfare and strategic arrangement of armies. He acquired thus wide knowledge besides his inherent intellectual calibre. He was convinced that the tyrannous and authoritative Mughal rule and *mullas'* communal bias were destroying the very texture of Indian life and her age-old traditions and thought. This brewed in him a commitment and determination to fight against these wrongs. There grew thus in him a religious leader, a soldier and other personality aspects. In pulpit he was a lawgiver, in battlefield a champion, in *masnada* a king commanding vast lands and subjects and in community of his Sikhs the humblest *faqir*. Hence, when he had the news of his father's ruthless murder and later his decollated head, he knew what he had to do.

Gobind Rai collected himself and began organising his Sikhs who were deeply hurt with the brutal killing of their supreme man, though they weren't broken. He concluded that sword, instead of his father's forgiveness or unresisting sacrifice, could better guard purity, righteousness, India's values, tradition, both social and religious, and the innocent countrymen against Islamic onslaught and oppression. The period from 1675 to 1683, but for his first marriage in 1677 and a war imposed on him in 1682 by Raja Bhim Chand of Kahlur, was almost a preparatory phase of his life.

The period from 1684 to 1690 is a phase of self-searching, introspection, enlightenment, and creativity. Most of his poetry which with his *Zafarnama* constituted *Dasam-granth*, belonged to these years. He was mostly at Paonta on Yamuna's banks shadowed by Himalayan peaks. Here

SAINT-SOLDIER GURU GOBIND SINGH
Sikh, Punjab, Modern, Oil on canvas, 64.5 x 43.5 cm
Artist: G.S. Sohan Singh, 1954
Collection: S.S. Hitkari, New Delhi
Rendered simply, yet the portrait depicts very powerfully Guru's intrinsic personality his thought and ideology. His face has an expression of divine solemnity and the softness of a child, and his eyes an expression of determination.

he revised the *Adi-granth* by adding to it a few verses of his father Guru Tegh Bahadur. But besides he fought two wars, one against Raja Bhim Chand who with rajas of Kangra and Guler attacked him, and the other against the confederation of the hill chiefs of Garhwal, Mandi, Bilaspur, Kotgrah, Hindur, Nurpur, Kangra, Guler and Kahlur. This war is known in history as Bhangini war and has great significance. The hill chiefs had developed a short of antipathy against him. They thought his military preparedness was against them.

The constant warfare, saint doing a soldier's job, marked the period from 1690 to 1699. The hill chiefs considered him a threat to their kingdoms and religious convictions. Besides they wanted to avenge the Bhangini defeat. They hence allied with Aurangzeb who was unhappy with him for he defied his supremacy and obstructed Islamic expansion. This resulted in constant Mughal pressure and recurring hill chiefs' attacks. Guru Gobind Rai fought during this period numerous battles, minor and major, some put their number to 42.

Guru Gobind Rai felt Sikhs, split and unorganised as they were, could not face the challenges they had before them. The worst was that they always needed someone to guide their personal and community life and command in wars. The incoherent Sikh movement, polluted by corrupt, detrimental and oppressive practices of *masands*, was seen head-

57

GURU GOBIND SINGH MEETING A SUFI SAINT
Mandi, Pahari, early 18th century
Paper, 14 x 20 cm, Acc. no: 47.110/354
Collection: National Museum, New Delhi.

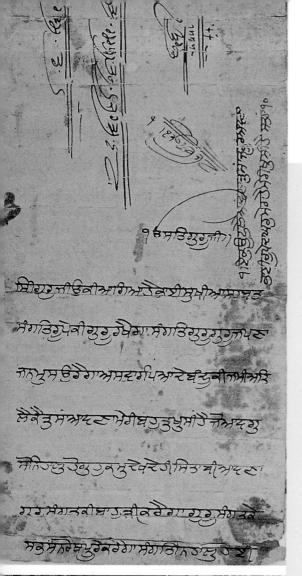

GURU GOBIND SINGH'S *HUKUM-NAMAH* TO
THE *SANGAT* OF VILLAGE BHAI RUPA
Paper, 23.5 x 11.7 cm, Script and language: Gurmukhi
Collection: Bhai Suchet Singh, village Bhai Rupa, Moga, Punjab
*This Hukum-nama dated August 2, 1696, addressed to the sangat of village Rupa,
expresses Guru Gobind Singh's full confidence in the sangat of the village. Considering
Bhai Rupa's house as his own the tenth Guru asked the sangat to reach the Guru-ghar
with soldiers, guns and camels. The Hukum-namah is signed by the Guruji himself.*

ing towards decay. Guru Gobind Rai foresaw further deterioration and misuse of Sikhs innocence by persons in authority. He hence sought to distinguish and organize such 'pure ones' as wished to form a community, distinct and committed to Nanak's path, adhering to a different code of conduct for individual as well as community life. The aim he set before him was thus three-fold, to identify the 'pure ones', to organise them into a community and to eradicate chances of corruption and misuse of religious authority. This three-fold object completely revolutionized Sikh movement and gave birth to its two most important events, birth of *Khalsa* and consecration of Sikhs' most sacred text the *Adi-granth* as their perpetual Guru replacing the one born of flesh and blood.

The birth of *Khalsa* aimed at identifying the 'pure ones,' and organizing them into a community with a distinction, inward and outward, in thinking and life style. Guru Gobind Rai devised a foolproof test. On Baisakhi in 1699 a huge congregation of Sikhs was held at Anandpur Sahib. Guru Gobind Rai emerged from his tent with a resolute face and a naked sword and announced that he needed the head of a Sikh and asked if anyone from the crowd would lay it under his sword. A deadly silence prevailed, but the very next moment one of them headed towards him. Guru Gobind Rai took him into the tent and within minutes returned with same resolute face and blood-stained sword. He repeated his call five times and each time one of his Sikhs offered him his head. After five rounds, Guru Gobind Rai finally came out the five supposed to have been decollated following him. Miracles ranked in Sikhism as blasphemy, many however inclined to believe that decollated ones were brought back to life by the Guru's supernatural powers.

This convinced Guru Gobind Rai that the flame of voluntary sacrifice which his father Guru Tegh Bahadur had lit was not yet extinct, and that the number of 'pure ones', the *Khalis*, was such as could be organized into a body. He proclaimed the body of such 'pure ones', would function as *Khalsa*, and its members would abide by certain codes of conduct and have a distinct identity, male names to have suffixed to them 'Singh' symbolizing lion's strength, stately grace and fearlessness, and female names 'Kaur' symbolizing purity. Members of *Khalsa* were required to lead a life of honesty, truthfulness, restraint, house hold, chastity and religion, and refrain from adultery and smoking. It was further prescribed that all male would wear on their persons a

A FOLIO FROM *DASAM-GRANTH (Close-up)*
Sikh, Punjab, circa A.D. 1860-70
Paper, 39 x 36 cm, Acc. no: 94.13
Collection: National Museum, New Delhi
*The compilation of the poetic works of the Tenth Guru,
this manuscript, the Dasam-Granth consists of
736 folios of which 40 are illustrated.*

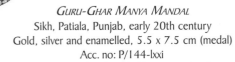

GURU-GHAR MANYA MANDAL
Sikh, Patiala, Punjab, early 20th century
Gold, silver and enamelled, 5.5 x 7.5 cm (medal)
Acc. no: P/144-lxxi
Collection: Sheesh Mahal Museum, Patiala
Inscription: Deg-Teg-Fateh-Sachche-Patshah
This medal with the portrait of Guru Gobind Singh was instituted
as an order of distinction by Maharaja Bhupinder Singh of Patiala.

Kangha, Kara, Kirpan, Kesh and *Kachcha*. The five who had offered their heads were the first members of *Khalsa*. In a huge vessel Guru Gobind Rai poured some water and stirred it with a *Khanda* and repeated during the process some verses and the five ones spoke:

Wah Guru ji ka Khalsa,
Wah Guru ji ki Fateh

The water in the vessel mixed with the might of *Khanda* and the spirit of *Gurbani* had become now *Amrit*, the nectar. He took on his palm a few drops and gave each of the five to drink. Specially favoured by the Guru they were called the *Panj Pyare*, the five beloved ones. Their names were changed to have with them 'Singh' as suffix. The *Khalsa* was installed and the five ones were the first baptized. With folded hands Guru Gobind Rai paid them his reverence and asked to baptize him.

With *Khalsa's* birth the Guruship was institutionalized all distinctions, caste, ranks or status vanishing. After Guruship merged into *Khalsa* the Guru and Sikhs were on par. Guru Gobind Rai, now Guru Gobind Singh, for he too was baptized, proclaimed *Khalsa* his own transformation:

Khalsa mero rup hai khas,
Khalse mein main Karun niwas.

He suggested that henceforth he were to be sought in this body of pure ones. He ruled any five Sikhs would be *Khalsa's* operative body. Incidentally, the beloved ones came from five different parts of the land and from five different castes representing all *varanas*. This made *Khalsa* from its very inception a community beyond caste, creed or race. Formerly baptizing to Sikhism was accomplished with water consecrated by dipping in it Guru's toe. It testified an entrant's humility. By replacing Guru's toe with *Khanda* the emphasis was shifted from humbleness to a Sikh's might, valour and courage, which the *Khanda* symbolized. Non-resisting passive resentment against tyranny, oppression and injustice were replaced by positive military action, though without deviating from the path of truth and justice, which made *Khalsa* a community of saint warriors. Guru ensured that a Sikh looked different, acted differently and was an entirely new personality with a new physiognomy, way of living and thinking, something which has ever since typified the Sikh and made him stand out conspicuously not only in India but all over the world.

Khalsa began channelising Sikh energy but in alike proportion mounted Mughal bias, and the enmity of hill chiefs, all

59

(Following page) KHANDA, THE STEEL WEAPON EDGED ON BOTH SIDES
Sikh, Punjab, early 19th century, Acc. no: 64/19-7-60
Collection: Qila Mubarak, Patiala
After the birth of Khalsa the Khanda symbolized to a Sikh, an instrument which transformed
by its touch simple water into nectar and thereby a simple folk into the purest one.
This Khanda was later made to crown the Nishan Sahib, and with a couple of swords,
or Kirpans, it has served now for three hundred years the Panth as its emblem.

unprovoked. They always joined hands against Sikhs. In 1704 Mughal forces assisted by hill states besieged Anandpur Sahib. The siege continued for long. Sikhs' arms and ammunition and stocks of eatables were almost all consumed. Advised by his mother and pressurised by the five beloved ones, one December night, full of stormy winds and torrenial rains and river Sarsa in full flood, Guru Gobind Singh left Anandpur Sahib. While crossing the river Guru's two younger sons and mother, betrayed by their own cook, were separated from him. The betrayer handed them over to the Nawab of Sirhand who, to win Aurangzeb's applause, crucified the children and their grandmother died of shock hearing the news. Guru Gobind Singh, with other part of his contingent, had hardly reached Chamkaur when they got the news of close proximity of the enemy army. They sought shelter in a mud house. Besides himself Guru Govind Singh had only 45 Sikhs including his two elder sons. Under a well-devised strategy he was able to keep the enemy engaged for a whole day though in the process he lost his 35 Sikhs including both his sons. Pressurized by the remaining ones Guru Govind Singh left Chamkaur with two Sikhs, but in an attempt to foil an enemy attack these two Sikhs too got

killed leaving the Guru alone to wander.

When Guru Govind Singh reached the jungles of Machhiwara, he was bare footed and clad in rags and if had anything to sate his acute thirst it was juice of Ak leaves. All tired and completely broken he lay under a tree. When in half slumber, Nabi Khan and Ghani Khan, his two former horse suppliers, passed thereby and recognised him. Despite the risk to their own lives they took him with them disguised as a *pir*. The Mughal army intercepted but a sufi affirming his identity as *Uch da pir* saved him. He was taken to Dina Kangarh. He stayed here for sometime and wrote *Zafar-Nama*, a letter in powerful Persian verse addressed to Aurangzeb. It was sent to the Mughal emperor. Here he collected a small contingent of Sikhs. After reading *Zafar-Nama* Aurangzeb's mind was completely changed. He sent words to his regional heads, but before his message reached them they had already attacked the Guru at Khidrana. Most of his Sikhs died in the battle. The wounded ones revealed their satisfaction to have served their Guru and thus attain salvation. At nearby Khidrana pond Guru Gobind Singh performed the last rites of dead and blessed their souls with salvation. The pond was renamed as Muktasar.

(Opposite page top) Guru Gobind Singh offering *Amrit* to *Panj-Piyare*
Sikh, Punjab, late 19th century
Paper, 28 x 20 cm, Acc. no: 2606
Collection: Govt. Museum and Art Gallery, Chandigarh
The painting depicts Guru Gobind Singh preparing Amrit with his
Khanda for baptizing to Khalsa his first five disciples known as Panj-Piyare.

(Opposite page bottom) Panj-Piyare
Children dressed as Panj-piyare for a procession on the occasion of Gurpurab.

ਸ੍ਰੀ ਗੁਰੂ ਗੋਬਿੰਦ ਸਿੰਘ ਜੀ
ਪਾਤਸਾਹੀ ੧੦

Greatly tired Guru Gobind Singh reached Talwandi Sabo. Here he had a somewhat peaceful phase to relax and rethink. The earlier copy of *Granth Sahib* was lost when he crossed river Sarsa. He decided to recompile and revise it for posterity, but those who had its other copies refused to give. He at last began compiling it out of his memory and surprising dictated to Bhai Mani Singh all 1430 pages of the Holy *Granth*.

Mughal prince Muazzam, who later ruled as Bahadur Shah I, realised that Mughals' understanding of Guru Gobind Singh was ill founded. He was hence somewhat friendly to him. He mediated a meeting between his father and Guru Gobind Singh. Aurangzeb was at that time at Aurangabad. Guru Gobind Singh hence left for Deccan with prince Muazzam to join him at Agra. But when on the way they had the news of Aurangazeb's death. Muazzam was required to return but Guru Gobind Singh preferred to proceed to Deccan. He reached Nanded. Here he foiled attempts of Banda Bairagi widely known for his great magic and supernatural powers. The subdued Banda Bairagi submitted to Guru's service. He is known to have served later great ends of Sikhism. When put to Punjab charge, he was the sole instrument to organise the split Sikhs to fight against re-

GURU GOBIND SINGH WITH HIS DISCIPLES
Sikh style with prominent Guler influence
Patiala, circa A.D. 1850-55
Paper, Acc. no: D/41
Collection: Sheesh Mahal Museum, Patiala

THE FOUR SONS OF GURU GOBIND SINGH
Sikh, Punjab, late 19th century
Paper, 30 x 21 cm, Acc. no: 2605
Collection: Govt. Museum and Art Gallery, Chandigarh
*The sons of Guru Gobind Singh like their father, attained the apex of martyrdom and
are hence as much revered in Sikh tradition. The two elder ones, sacrificed their lives
in the battle of Chamkaur and the two younger ones, betrayed by their own aide were masoned
alive into a wall and ruthlessly crucified by the Mughal subedar of Sirhind.*

cently erupted disturbances and Sikhs oppression.

At Nanded Guru Gobind Singh gave to the Sikh tradition its another great institution, the Guru in the immortal body of the *Granth*, the *Sri Guru Granth Sahib* to guide Sikhs in all future and in all eventualities. He aimed at enabling Sikhs to enlighten themselves with the divine knowledge which *Sri Guru Granth Sahib* imparted and discover a proper course in life and seek salvation after it. In his attempt to eradicate chances of corruption, misuse of authority, vices and perversions to which human flesh usually proned he sought eternal knowledge embodied in the sacred *Granth* to be Sikh's perpetual Guru, uniform, non-erosive, incorruptible and timeless. He was stabbed by a traitor, a Pathan, attending his congregation everyday and thereby winning his confidence. But before the *jot*, the flame, merged with the *akhanda jot*, the eternal fire, Guru Gobind Singh performed as Sikh Guru his last rite but, perhaps, more significant than founding *Khalsa*. He took five paisa and a coconut into his hands and placing them upon the Holy *Granth*, prostrated before it and proclaimed that the Holy *Granth* would henceforth lead and guide the *Khalsa* and would command Sikhs as their Guru and was then onward their Guru, the *Sri Guru Granth Sahib*.

THE LAST JOURNEY OF GURU GOBIND SINGH
Sikh–Pahari mix style, circa A.D. 1800
Paper, 17 x 28 cm, Acc. no: 3491
Collection: Govt. Museum and Art Gallery, Chandigarh
*This painting symbolically depicts how foreseeing his end approaching close
Guru Gobind Singh, to meet the Akal Purakha, got a pyre
prepared and proceeded on his horse to it led or assisted by none.*

Transcribing the Great Vision

Risen to the great vision and massive spiritual strength Punjab was, thus, reborn. The great tradition of Indus man seeking life's totality had begun crystallizing despite upheavals, uncertainties and several counter factors. It had been led to its all time perfection and accomplishment by the Sikh Gurus. But it was not all. It continued to sustain for many who had an eye for the divine vision, other than the great Gurus, incessantly put their efforts, however meagre, to advance and consolidate it.

What Nanak's songs breathed into this tradition was doubled by Mardana's *rabbab* accompanying his songs, the one lending to it its breath and the other its blood, vigour and vibrations. Though a mere disciple, he shared with his Guru the same divine impulse and his lyre rose to same spiritual fervour which Nanak's songs inspired. Absolute submission, a sort of dissolution of one's being into the Supreme whom the Guru represented, and the singleness of mind and aim, besides his enchanting and spirited music, were Mardana's attributes which the tradition borrowed from him for casting some of its great ideals. Baba Buddhaji, who applied *tilaks* to five Sikh Gurus, was amongst the earliest ones to join Nanak's path. The humble Buddhaji, a Sikh to the last, was the model of unique contentment. Sikhism discovered the ideals of complacence, unflickering devotion and

BHAI MARDANA (1459-1534)
Sikh, Punjab, Modern, Oil on canvas, 18" x 23.5"
Artist: Kirpal Singh, 1976
Collection: Punjab and Sind Bank, New Delhi
The rabbab was Mardana's constant companion as he himself was that of Guru Nanak.
The artist in this painting has sought his identity in his rabbab.

64

(Below) MAI BHAGO
Sikh, Punjab, Modern, Oil on canvas
Artist: Kirpal Singh, 1974
Collection: Punjab and Sind Bank, New Delhi
*Mai Bhago was deeply devoted to Guru Gobind Singh, fighting in
male attire at Khidrana in 1705, now known as Muktsar.*

service in Buddhaji's adherence to *Panth* and in his selfless service.

Sri Guru Granth Sahib, with the *shabad*:

> *Balwanda Kiwi nekjan jis
> bahuti chhau pratrayi,
> Langar daulat wandian rasa
> amrit khir ghilayi,*

itself underlines the contribution of Guru Angad's consort Mata Kiwi who imparted to *langar* the sanctity and status of a sacred and one of the most important institutions of Sikhism. The *shabad* acclaims that the *langar* tasted as *amrit*, the nectar, whenever Mata Kiwi served it. It suggested that the *langar*, after it had been institutionalized, was the prime instrument and source that immortalised and perpetuated the Sikh tradition. Bibi Bhani, the daughter of Guru Amardas, chose to remain in her father's service till his last. By

deviating from the earlier position where it was only a son's prerogative to remain in father's service, she brought about a drastic change and earned for daughter son-like right to serve her parents.

Mata Ganga, the wife of Guru Arjan, played important role in supervising and custodying the *banis* collected for compiling *Adigranth*. Guru Gobind Singh's mother, Mata Gujari, was for her son a great protective umbrella, and perpetual source of inspiration. Mai Bhago, Guru Gobind Singh's great devotee, fought for him several times in male disguise. The Tenth Guru's wife Mata Sundari, after Guruji's death, led and guided for long years the *Panth* and *Khalsa*. Balwanda, one of Mardana's two sons, composed a lot of poetry dedicated to Gurus' praise and God's worship. *Sri Guru Granth Sahib* includes two of his verses. It was Bhai Gurdas

(Top right) BIBI BHANI-THE CONSORT OF GURU RAMDAS
Jaipur style, Rajasthan, mid 18th century, Paper, 17 x 13 cm
Collection: Bhai Suchet Singh, village Bhai Rupa, Moga, Punjab

(Right) BABA BUDDHAJI
Sikh, Punjab, Modern, Oil on canvas, 24 x 18.5 cm, Artist: Bodhraj, 1976
Collection: Punjab and Sind Bank, New Delhi
*He served the Panth unaspiringly and gave to Sikhism the ideals
of complacence and unflickering devotion and service.*

who, dictated by Guru Arjan, inscribed the holy *Adi-granth*. Bhai Gurdas also composed numerous *varan*, though none of them got a place in the sacred Book, for whatever reasons.

The cult of serving the wounded at war beyond distinctions of caste, creed or nationality, a pure humanism as represents Red Cross today, emerged into Sikh tradition from the spirit of Sikh volunteers serving war victims. The spirit touched its heights in Bhai Kanhaiya, a devotee of Guru Teg Bahadur and later that of Guru Gobind Singh but in battlefield a friend of all wounded needing help. Once during 1705 siege of Anandpur Sahib Guru Gobind Singh received a complaint that Bhai Kanhaiya served water even to wounded Mughal soldiers. He was summoned. Quiet was his answer. He said he fed neither a Mughal, a Sikh, nor a Hindu; he only served the wounded. Guru Gobind Singh, it is said, declared that Kanhaiya was one who had rightly apprehended the essence of *Panth* and his teachings.

Banda Bahadur, Guru Gobind Singh's nominee, was sent to Punjab by him just before his death at Nanded with five arrows, a drum, banner and five Sikhs, as emblem of his authority. He reorganised split Sikhs, revived and upheld *Khalsa* and brought under it the entire Punjab from Yamuna to Sutlej, the total area yielding revenue of Rs. thirty six lacs, though not for long. He captured Lahore and issued in Nanak's name a silver coin and a calendar to commence since. His first victims were the Nawab of Sirhind and the killer of Guru's infant sons.

He led Sikhs with great ability, boosted their morale and revived their confidence in the community of *Khalsa*. He re-iterated

(Top left) BHAI MANJH
Sikh, Punjab, Modern, Oil on canvas
Artist: Devender Singh
Collection: Punjab and Sind Bank, New Delhi
An ardent disciple of Guru Arjan, he used to bring dry wood for langar everyday.
One day while carying wood he tumbled into a well and despite his predicament,
Bhai ji saved the wood from getting wet.

the ideals of Sikhism in his deeds during his short span. He made tillers masters of lands they cultivated, placed even Muslims in several high positions and allowed all to follow freely their own faiths. After a long siege when Farukhsiyar, the Mughal emperor, arrested him with other 740 Sikhs, he laid his life adhering to the great Sikh tradition of sacrifice, but flinched not from the path of righteousness. History records the unbelievable acts of imperial brutalities. Every day a hundred of his Sikhs were butchered from limb to limb and piece to piece, in his very presence and the last day his own four year son but Banda Bahadur maintained a saint's composure and did not falter from his path.

When Guru Gobind Singh waded his way militarily through antipathies, disasters and recurring enemy action, there were his Sikhs and devotees engaged in sustaining the tradition by other creative means, drawing their inspiration mainly from the life and writings of Guru Gobind Singh himself. Besides the Punjab's folks, *varan*, or ballads, depicting Tenth Guru's chivalry and sacrifice and the Sikh ideals sung all over, poets like Senapati, Bhai Nand Lal etc. carried to masses Guru Gobind Singh's deeds and *Panth's* message. Bhai Nand Lal, writing as Goya, alone came out with several poetic works devoted to depict Sikh tradition and Guru Gobind Singh's life, some of the important ones being *Zindaginama*, *Rahatnama*, *Diwan-i-Goya* and *Rubaiyat-i-Goya*. The great tradition thus continued to sustain. When eventualities lulled the Sikh sword and guns, the pen strove to uphold it on paper and the throat in its songs and echoes.

Antipathies constantly sought to erode the Sikh tradition, but Sikhs and *Khalsa* put alike efforts

(Top centre) JASSA SINGH RAMGARHIA WITH JODH SINGH AND BIR SINGH
Sikh–Pahari mix style, late 18th century
Attributed to the artist Purkhu of Kangra
Paper, 16.5 x 21 cm, Acc. no: 60.543
Collection: National Museum, New Delhi
Under the able leadership of Jassa Singh Ahluwalia and Ramgarhia the Sikhs organised
themselves and completed the re-construction of Hari Mandir by 1776.

Hukam Nama of Banda Bahadur to Bhai Dharam
and Param Singh of village Bhai Rupa
Sikh, Punjab, early 18th century, Paper, 16 x 10.5 cm
Script: Gurmukhi, Language: Punjabi
Collection: Bhai Suchet Singh, village Bhai Rupa, Punjab
It contains on it the mohar, seal, conceived by Banda Bahadur
and widely used later in Sikh coinage
Deg Teg Fateh nusrat-i-bedrang, Yaft az Nanak Guru Gobind Singh.

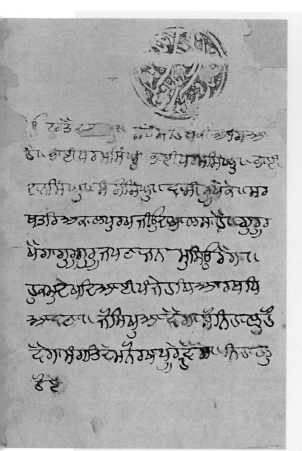

to protect, strengthen and rebuild it. After Harimandir was the principal seat of Guruship with the Holy Granth presiding as *Panth's* Guru, it came in greater focus of plunderers and invaders. It was recurrently damaged by sectarian antipathies but in 1764 was almost completely demolished by Ahmed Shah Abdali. For its repair financial assistance used to reach from various Sikh chiefs but this time it was somewhat different. Putting aside the mutual confrontations all Sikh chiefs confederated under Sardar Jassa Singh Ahluwalia and undertook the re-construction of the holy shrine. It was accomplished by 1776. The Sikh unity so arrived at perpetuated at least on sectarian agenda. The security of Harimandir was accepted as a joint responsibility of all.

Baba Baghel Singh is credited to carry beyond Punjab the flag of Sikhs, the Sikh power and Sikh architecture, an instrument of commemorating the unprecedented sacrifices of Sikh Gurus and a means perpetuating their great message. When Shah Alam, the Mughal emperor, ruled Delhi, Baba Baghel Singh with a strong contingent of forty thousand strong Sikhs, marching via Saharanpur, reached the Mughal capital and hoisted at Red Fort the flag of *Khalsa*. Shah Alam, weak as he was, moved to negotiate with Baba Baghel Singh and a treaty was

signned, but from Baba Baghel Singh's side neither for any ransom nor for territories. He demanded for transferring to Sikhs the sites of Sikh importance and license enabling them to build their commemorative holy shrines. The sites where stand now Gurdwaras Rakabganj, Sheehganj, Bala Sahib, Bangla Sahib, Motibagh, Teliwara and Mujnubagh were identfed and transferred to Sikhs, and within a record period of just eight months Baba Baghel Singh constructed there seven lofty Gurdwaras.

Many more related to different areas, though history forgot to mention them, have contributed for sustaining and promoting the Sikh tradition. Many traders and common men financed and patronised activities that helped uphold the Sikh cause, though in the face of feudal antipathy they seem to have kept themselves aloof from the eye of history and record. This is evidenced from numerous copies of the holy text with some quite expensive and the Sikh shrines scattered all over obviously built by local people. The National Museum, New Delhi has in its collection an ambitious large size illustrated copy of the sacred *Sri Guru Granth Sahib* painted using a good amount of gold. A copy similar to it, by the same scribe, artist and patron, is in the possession of the former jagirdar of

(Previous page right top) Bhai Kanhaiya
serving water to wounded soldiers
Sikh, Punjab, Modern, Oil on canvas, Artist: Kirpal Singh, 1974
Collection: Punjab and Sind Bank, New Delhi

(Previous page second from top) The Sikh warriors
Sikh, Punjab, Modern, Oil on canvas, 46" x 35"
Artist: Kirpal Singh, 1963, Acc. no: 3184
Collection: Govt. Museum and Art Gallery, Chandigarh.

Bagarian in Nabha district. Some Sodhi Bhan Singh partonised both these copies, though there is nothing in record to identify him. Presumably there would have been several like Sodhi Bhan Singh who constantly perpetuated the *Panth* and Gurus' message though always in a low profile.

The later Punjab, its life-form, civil and folk, literature, arts, crafts, music, architecture, both sectarian and domestic, trade and industries, customs and costumes, polity, social set-up, ecclesiastic management, rituals, religious outlook, thought and ideologies, ethical values, worldly view and spiritualism, aspirations, zeal to grow and fight out to a goal all reflect in them this unique legacy which defines itself as Sikhism, the mighty and the massive tradition evolved out of the three hundred years of Sikh movement which the Sikh Gurus guided with their divine strength, force of personal character, the unique courage, the adherence to truth, and the exceptional self-restraint, great humanism, ideals of universal love, fraternity and equality, great nationhood and appalling sacrifice, besides each one form Guru Nanak to Guru Gobind Singh contributing to it something of his own, novel, typical and different.

Everything in Punjab, or anywhere in the life of a Sikh, reveals some ascertainable relevance to this tradition. These three hundred years of Punjab, after Guru Gobind Singh, have such deep impact of this tradition that the past appears to have extended into the present. They have hardly ever deviated from the earlier position, its sanctions and taboos

(Opposite page bottom) CHAKRA, THE SET OF RINGS USED
AROUND THE TURBAN BY *NIHANGS*
Sikh, Punjab, early 19th century, Dia: 17 cm, Acc. no: 81/1 to 4
Collection: Qila Mubarak, Patiala.

(Above) A NIHANG AT THE HOLY *SAROVAR*, AMRITSAR
Lithograph by William Simpson, 1859-62
Paper, 30.5 x 20.5 cm
Collection: Hotel Imperial, New Delhi.

remaining as much in reverence. Sikhism did not approve from its very inception iconolatry and hence even modern Sikh artist's refrain from seeking the Sikh Gurus or their idea of the 'divine' in iconographic representations. Sculpture, both independently rendered or as part of temple or shrine architecture, remain a weak point of Punjab Art Movement. Even visual representations were little approved with the result that portrayal of Gurus' personal likenesses in independent portrait form came in vogue quite late, sometimes at the end of the 18th century. Though through the illustrations of the *Adi-granth* and the *Janam-sakhis* the depiction of Gurus' likenesses and their life-

events had begun in the 17th century itself when approved by some later Gurus even their independent portraits were rendered.

It was only during the reign of the Sikh ruler Maharaja Ranjit Singh that, encouraged and approved by him, Sikh artists rendered Gurus' personal likenesses and life-events on a larger scale not only on canvas but on several unconventional articles like weapons, shields, medals and ornaments, and, of course, on walls and roofs of shrines and palaces. By transcribing Guru's, ideals and life-models into visuals on arte-facts, both weapons, crowns and ornaments and the articles of day-to-day use, Maharaja Ranjit Singh sought to

perpetuate Gurus' memories, Sikh ideals and the Sikh movement, and at the same time by inspiring a feeling of divine presence and participation in whatever they did or wherever they were, he led the house-holders to keep along the path of righteousness and the soldiers to realise that they were *dharma-yoddhas* fighting for Gurus' divine cause and for a great mission. The feeling that they had Gurus' weapons in their hands, besides that such weapons ensured a soldier's identity, boosted their morale, inspired in them spiritual strength, valour and a zeal to make any sacrifice and worked as clutches refraining them from erring and wrong doing.

(Top) A GOLD NECKLACE
Collection: Toshakhana, Golden Temple, Amritsar
*This necklace with the portrait of Baba Nanak on its pendant
is an excellent example of Sikh artefacts, a tradition initiated
and popularised by Maharaja Ranjit Singh.
This gold necklace is believed to have been donated by him to Golden Temple.*

Maharaja Ranjit Singh

◆

MAHARAJA RANJIT SINGH IN PROCESSION
Sikh, Punjab, mid 19th century
Paper, 30 x 22.5 cm, Acc. no: IS282-1955
Collection: Victoria & Albert Museum, London, UK.

Maharaja Ranjit Singh, born in 1780, outstands in entire Sikh history as the mightiest instrument purgating the life of Punjab by infusing into it the great divine vision and by perpetuating the great legacy of Sikhism. Incidentally after a hundred years of its birth *Khalsa* found in Maharaja Ranjit Singh its all time base, means to both, revive and survive, and regal cover and patronage to grow and expand. His liberal and broad-based outlook, reverence for all religions alike and an all-embracing policy made Sikhism more acceptable. He eradicated what precipitated in past antipathy against Sikhism and won people's favour not by might of sword but by his just rule, state's patronage, genuineness, love and equal regard for all. He championed larger interests but keeping Sikh interests a little above the rest.

He widened the horizons of Sikhism, gave it a wider geography, larger followings and broader vision. He brought it down to the soil, from a few to many, a consecrated place to a housewife's kitchen, a farmer's furrow, a youth's marriage and a newborn's birth rites. Several forbidden or semi-forbidden things were allowed to prevail, though within the frame of Sikhism. Iconographic representations

KAUKAB-I-PUNJAB, OR THE BRIGHTEST STAR OF PUNJAB
Sikh, Punjab, dated A.D. 1838, 8 x 5 cm
Collection: Sheesh Mahal Museum, Patiala
Its obverse consists of a circle with a gold frame housing in it a portrait of Maharaja Ranjit Singh and ten petals around studded with precious diamonds. The circle on the reverse contains inside it the motif of flowering plant consisting of enamel-work. The five larger leaves too contain similar, though smaller, plant motifs. The crowning base against which the star suspends is in lehariya design. The fabulous use of gold, diamonds and other precious stones set and enamelled marks the star with great magnificence. Maharaja Ranjit Singh presented this medal to the then Governor General of India, Lord Auckland.

THE PORTRAIT OF MAHARAJA RANJIT SINGH
Sikh, Punjab, mid 19th century
Paper, 24.5 x 17.5 cm, Acc. no: 91.11
Collection: National Museum, New Delhi.

weren't yet allowed, but relief iconography, Gurus' portraits carved on shields, medals, pendants, handles of swords and other weapons and on several other items of day-to-day use, came to prevail in vogue. Portrait painting, especially what represented Gurus and the royal family, was highly favoured. It was when Maharaja Ranjit Singh had several European friends visiting him. They had brought with them the cult of portrait painting and some of them even portrayed Maharaja Ranjit Singh. This greatly influenced Sikh art and related activities bearing a creative climate and art consciousness.

Piri and *Miri*, or soldier-saint concept had long back evolved

(Top right) THE ORDER OF MAHARAJA RANJIT SINGH
Sikh, Punjab, circa A.D. 1835-38, 7.5 x 4.4 cm, Acc. no: P/73-III
Collection: Sheesh Mahal Museum, Patiala

The centre of the medal consists of a circle, with the portrait of Maharaja Ranjit Singh cast in gold, and sun like radiating six petals dividing the zodiac into twelve zones by its angular rays. The outer space consists of six leaves, three enamelled with white, red and blue, the two of the rest are covered by images of ferocious bulls and the third with an eagle perched on a naked sword. Maharaja has been portrayed quite young and with a resolute face. The names of the three important campaigns of the Maharaja Mankhera, Multan and Kashmir and Peshawar, are inscribed on these leaves on the reverse. Alike the circle on the reverse has a Persian inscription "Maharaja Ranjit Singh Bahadur walli-e-Punjab".

in Sikh tradition, however a sovereign's reverence for Sikh Gurus deeply motivated artists to paint them with greater regalia, nimbus, crown, or bejewelled *Kalagi*, throne, and splendour around. It seems hawk was an artistic innovation introduced with Guru Gobind Singh's portrayal during this period for symbolising his imperial status for it otherwise did not befit the personality of the great Guru who aimed at nurturing birds to such might as could undo the hawk. Hawk to him had symbolised tyranny and birds the common humble masses. The liberal attitude of Maharaja Ranjit Singh encouraged literature other than religious, the chronological, fictional, romantic and also the secular art

and crafts. Textiles came to depict divine likenesses, portraits of Gurus, their life-events and also the sacred text, especially the *Mul-Mantra*, though not such textiles, which were used as costumes. The *rumalas* used for covering Sri Guru Granth Sahib and sheets lying under the sacred *Granth* were usually embroidered and painted with holy text and Gurus' portraits. Maharaja Ranjit Singh had exceptional liking for shawls promoting their use as means of financial exchange, for realizing taxes and paying fees and revenues. These shawls were usually embroidered with Sikh motifs and reflected Sikh heritage. The life in Punjab had become under Maharaja Ranjit Singh the mirror of Sikhism.

In 1790, when 10, Ranjit Singh lost his father, encumbering his childhood with the responsibility of managing his father's Misl, the Sukkarchakkia. Though he had the benign regency of his mother Rajkaur guiding and protecting him, yet the volcano that the infighting Sikh powers and the split chieftains and rulers of small principalities precipitated in Punjab was not any less explosive. The split Punjab, from Yamuna to Sutlej, comprising of numerous small *thikanas* and Misls headed by Sikh, Rajput, Pathan and Muslim chiefs, usually engaged in mutual warfare, craved for consolidation and to regain its identity, which befitted its great legacy. The dominions of *Khalsa*— Multan, Bahawalpur, Derajat,

(Following page) AN ENGRAVED SWORD
Sikh, Punjab, early 19th century, 61 cm
Gold and steel, Acc. no: 56/19
Collection: Qila Mubarak, Patiala
The blade is rendered with figures of Baba Nanak, Bhai Bala and Mardana, alongwith motifs of the lion, running deer, makara and two birds. The hilt is decorated with the figures of Ganesha, Shiva, Bhagwati and Krishna. All figures are heavily cast and polished in gold. The sword's size indicates that it was meant for someone young.

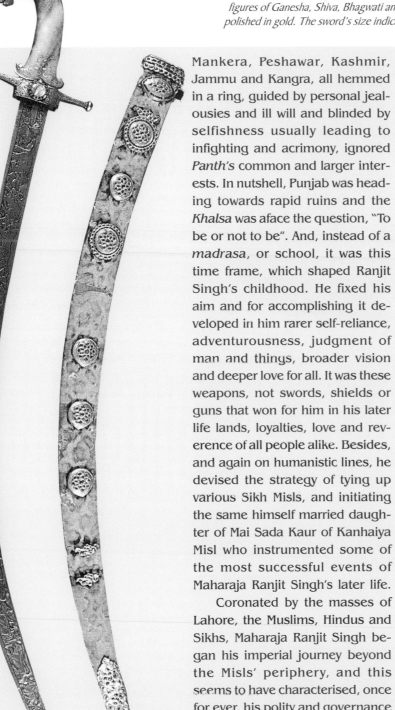

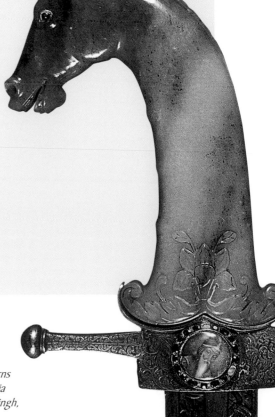

Mankera, Peshawar, Kashmir, Jammu and Kangra, all hemmed in a ring, guided by personal jealousies and ill will and blinded by selfishness usually leading to infighting and acrimony, ignored *Panth's* common and larger interests. In nutshell, Punjab was heading towards rapid ruins and the *Khalsa* was aface the question, "To be or not to be". And, instead of a *madrasa*, or school, it was this time frame, which shaped Ranjit Singh's childhood. He fixed his aim and for accomplishing it developed in him rarer self-reliance, adventurousness, judgment of man and things, broader vision and deeper love for all. It was these weapons, not swords, shields or guns that won for him in his later life lands, loyalties, love and reverence of all people alike. Besides, and again on humanistic lines, he devised the strategy of tying up various Sikh Misls, and initiating the same himself married daughter of Mai Sada Kaur of Kanhaiya Misl who instrumented some of the most successful events of Maharaja Ranjit Singh's later life.

Coronated by the masses of Lahore, the Muslims, Hindus and Sikhs, Maharaja Ranjit Singh began his imperial journey beyond the Misls' periphery, and this seems to have characterised, once for ever, his polity and governance and, to a great extant, his view on life, art, literature and even Sikhism. In his cult of equality,

social justice and parity in all matters whatsoever, reverence for all faiths alike, preservation of past, protection of antiquity, and in his rule of law he was till end people's champion, a democrat in the truest sense. And, in this consisted his vision of Sikhism and a reflection of the legacy of the people of Lahore, who tired of foreign invasions, after receiving the news of Nizam-ud-din of Kasur advancing towards Lahore, jointly sent to Ranjit Singh a petition for their protection from the invader. As their champion, on 7th July, 1799 he entered Lahore and made it his seat. It proved a great turning point in the life of Maharaja Ranjit Singh but of as much magnitude in the life of

75

(Above and right) THE SWORD OF MAHARAJA RANJIT SINGH
Sikh, Punjab, early 19th century, 104.5 x 14 cm
Collection: Maharaja Ranjit Singh Museum, Amritsar
The sword contains on its blade various hunting scenes, on quillon delicate patterns in gold and, on its ivory central base the portrait of Maharaja studded with rubies and on scabbard various patterns created with eleven gold pieces, precious stones and emeralds. This sword was gifted by the Maharaja to Capt. Brown Roberts from whom it passed on to some antique dealer of London. Later Bhupinder Singh, Maharaja Patiala bought it from that London dealer and brought it back to India. After Independence his son Maharaja Yadavinder Singh presented it to the Govt. of Punjab.

Sikhism for it found in Ranjit Singh, save the divine Ten Gurus, its ever-greatest champion and benefactor.

Soon after 1799 Ranjit Singh concentrated on expanding and consolidating his empire. Jammu was targeted first and was let out only after its chief offered him huge gifts. Small states like Sialkot and Mirowal fell to him in consequence. Several other chiefs owed him allegiance. Recognition followed from abroad, states like Hyderabad and Kabul, and powers like the East India Company and many others sending him presents, felicitations and a hand of friendship. Now almost entire Punjab was under him, the first Sikh ruler begot by Punjab's soil to rule his own land. People's love and esteem for him prevailed, and on 12th April, 1801, in a splendid *darbar* at Lahore they crowned him as the Maharaja of Punjab, a direct descendant of Guru Nanak, Baba Sahib Singh Bedi, applying the *tilak* on his forehead. Maharaja Ranjit Singh preferred, though, till last to be called Sarkar instead, in view that the Guru alone was the real King, the *Sachcha Patshah*.

Different religious sections of his subjects, Muslims, Hindus, Europeans and Sikhs, would be governed by their own religious, sectarian and personal laws was one of his earliest proclamations. This marked a transition from the prior theocratic rule to the present day secular statehood the seeds of which Maharaja Ranjit Singh had in "*Na koi Hindu, na koi Musalman*" concept of Sikhism. He thus drew a bridge between the Sikh tradition and the modernism, which he was able to foresee. Not merely in ideology but true to the Sikh tradition and teachings of Sikh Gurus he unhesitatingly placed his government and all his resources into the hands of both alike, Hindus and Muslims, and, of course, the Sikhs. If he discriminated anything it was always the 'talent from communalism and nepotism'.

This typically simple Punjabi, almost a rustic in his habits, who had no formal education and hardly able to write his name and issuing Farmans with the impression of his palm, had Mughal emperor Akbar-like wisdom and love for knowledge, arts, crafts, literature, architecture, greenery, gardens, music, dance, monuments, antiquity, and all that was sacred, beautiful and great. He struck a balance in everything. Persian was the language of his court and record and Punjabi of the conversation and dialogue with his people at large. He gave liberal grants to them who imparted education in Gurmukhi and Sanskrit. He himself could neither write nor read, yet when read out to him he could revise or modify a Persian draft in Persian itself and a Punjabi in Punjabi.

Three Faqir brothers, Faqir Syed Azizuddin, Nuruddin and Imamuddin, Pandit Dinanath and Raja Dhiyan Singh were all alike strong pillars of his kingdom and were alike esteemed by Maharaja Ranjit Singh. His dialogue with them and with various visitors, travellers, emissaries and representatives of other countries and

(Opposite page) A PORCELAIN JAR
Collection: S. Atamjit Singh Vegha, Dehradun
This jar portraying Ten Sikh Gurus is a Japanese production from the Satsuma Faience works whose company Mark is given on the base of the object. The jar is dated 1875. It was acquired in 1968 by the collector from a dealer of Bombay who purchased it in an auction at Hyderabad. It is believed that the same must have been prepared for Cis-Satluj states, particularly for the former state of Nabha.

states and agents of East India Company widened his knowledge, broadened his consciousness and developed his insight besides his own inborn intelligence and talent. He sought the assistance of Capt. Wade, Company's agent at Ludhiana, in translating English Penal Code and got translated Mulla Hussain's Persian classic *Anwar-i-Suheli* in *Brajbhasha* by Budh Singh for the guidance of his courtiers, officers, princes, chiefs and rajas. When Sikh army raided Peshawar in 1834, he commanded Hari Singh Nalwa, the army commander, that the library of Hazrat Omar Sahib was to be left safe.

Maharaja Ranjit Singh liberally patronised writing, whatever its language or theme, though Persian was greater in vogue. On his instance were composed several manuscripts, some of the important ones being *Zafarnama-i-Ranjit Singh* by Diwan Amar Nath, the son of Pandit Dina Nath, *Tawarikh-i-Punjab* by the known Persian scholar of his time Ghulam Muhayy-ud-din, popularly known as Bute Shah, and the *Umdat-ul-Tawarikh*, again in Persian, by Sohan Lal Suri, the court diarist of Maharaja Ranjit Singh. It thus created a climate wherein Sikhs and Hindus were seen

taking up Islamic themes and legends, and Muslim writers Hindu and Sikh themes and legends perpetuating thereby a culture, beyond sectional, communal, sectarian, or feudalistic considerations, the culture of Hindustan. And, undoubtedly not only in the good qualities of his heart and head but also in the root of this wide cultural concept the *Sri Guru Granth Sahib* was his inherent source and inspiration.

The great vision, thus, manifested itself in life's totality in Punjab interweaving with the material texture the essence of spiritualism minimising what disintegrated and bred antipathy and strengthening that which united and sustained. Maharaja Ranjit

Singh struck silver and copper coins and named them *Nanak-shahi* suggesting that Guru Nanak was the supreme Shah. Coins' one side had engraved on it the portrait of Guru Nanak and the other was inscribed with '*Guru Nanak Sahai*', both in Persian and *Gurmukhi*. Some of these coins repeated the inscription that Banda Bahadur had used on his coins when he had captured Lahore:

'*Deg-o-tegh-o-fateh-o-Nusrat Bedirang,*
Yaft az Nanak Guru Gobind Singh.'

These coins acclaimed Maharaja Ranjit Singh's political sovereignty, supreme benefaction of

(Below) A VELVET SHAWL WITH PORTRAITS OF TEN SIKH GURUS EMBROIDERED IN GOLD
Sikh, Punjab, early 20th century, Velvet and thread
A characteristic Kashmir Sikh shawl, an art tradition originated in the valley but brought to
Punjab plains for a greater thrust and viability during the reign of Maharaja Ranjit Singh.

(Right and bottom right) A COPPER COIN
Sikh, Punjab, early 19th century
Collection: National Museum, New Delhi
On the obverse fragments of the words Akal Sahai and Nanakji can be easily read.

78

Guru Nanak and served as standard of exchange and trade, that was, a coin was made to belong to the three realms, Gurus' spiritual realm, the sovereign's political realm and common man's trade and commerce. In everything Maharaja Ranjit Singh was able to visualise what belonged to the divine, to the political authority and to the commonalty. He was gifted a marvellous gilded gold canopy by the Nizam of Hyderabad as a token of friendship. It was too precious for a man to keep and could only belong to the divine. Maharaja Ranjit Singh hence immediately sent it to Sri Harmandir Sahib. In everything he infused spirituality and everything revealed to him an aspect which was other than the material one.

A building's relevance to Ma-haraja Ranjit Singh was not in its mere sectarian or purposive context. He was able to see its antiqueness and monumentality and considered it state's responsibility to protect and preserve. Accordingly, buildings built by Jahangir and Shahjahan were repaired and maintained at the expenses from state. A portion of the enclosure of the tomb of Shah Bilawal had been swept away by river Ravi. Lest the rest of the tomb met the same fate Maharaja Ranjit Singh built for his remains a new tomb at a safer site and got them shifted to this new abode. The samadhi of Guru Arjan at Lahore was almost rebuilt with a fine edifice added over it. The Hazuri Bagh at Lahore was added with a beautiful *baradari*, and at Amritsar the Rambagh was laid

(Above right) THE BOND OF TREATY EXECUTED BETWEEN MAHARAJA RANJIT SINGH
AND RAJA FATEH SINGH OF KAPURTHALA
Sikh, Punjab, A.D. 13.4.1827
Paper, 26 x 13.5 cm, Acc. no: 9
Collection: Maharaja Ranjit Singh Museum, Amritsar
It contains the impression of Maharaja's palm in saffron
which he had used as his signatures on this treaty.

with another alike beautiful one. The Sikh element marked the new buildings as well. The house he built at Lahore had splendid display of arabesques, glass-work and stucco embellished with floral designs, foliages, vine and vase patterns similar to the patterns of Sri Harmandir Sahib. It was a Sikh transcription of the Islamic idiom. His other building known as Sheesh Mahal, built at Wazirabad, had fine wall paintings portraying Sikh Gurus and illustrating various Sikh themes. In Maharaja Ranjit Singh's building activities reflected both, the elements of Sikh architecture and his own cult and craving for antiquity and monumentality, but in his constant service and care of Sri Harmandir Sahib, its total interior renovated with finely incised marble and exterior covered with the plates and leaves of gold giving the sacred building its Golden Temple name, reflected his deep devotion to God's house and his incessant prayer to the Supreme.

MAHARAJA RANJIT SINGH PROCEEDING ON *BASANT PANCHAMI* CELEBRATIONS
Sikh, Punjab, mid 19th century
Paper, 23.6 x 18 cm, Acc. no: 3305
Collection: Govt. Museum and Art Gallery, Chandigarh
*Record reveals that Maharaja Ranjit Singh used to go to the sacred tomb of Lal Hussain at Lahore for
participating in Basant Panchami celebrations. Heavily bejewelled Maharaja is in yellow costume, all his attendants and
even his galloping horse in beautiful yellow cover, golden saddles and yak tail's puff all reflecting Basant mood.*

AN ILLUSTRATION OF RAM BAGH PALACE COMPLEX
from the Persian manuscript *Gulgasht-i-Punjab*
Sikh, Punjab, dated 1849 A.D.
Paper, 36 x 22.5 cm, Acc. no: 7
Collection: Maharaja Ranjit Singh Museum, Amritsar.

82

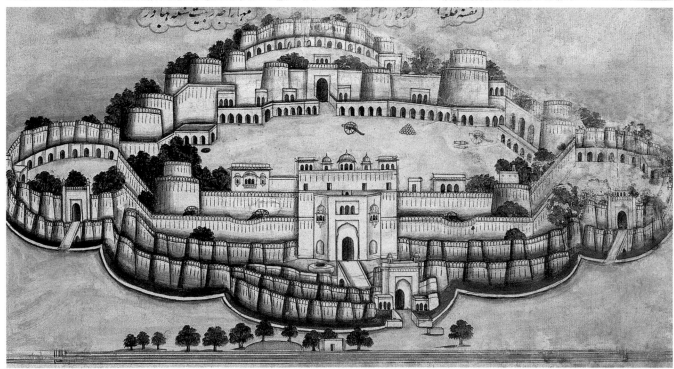

GOBINDGARH FORT
Sikh, Punjab, mid 19th century
Paper, 20.5 x 34.5 cm, Acc. no: 85.26
Collection: National Museum, New Delhi.

The Great Legacy

History records a Sikh soldier saying, "Today Ranjit Singh is dead", after Maharaja Ranjit Singh's 1809 Amritsar treaty of 'perpetual friendship' with the British. Maharaja Ranjit Singh was a dream manifest. It dreamt of a compact National monarchy with Sikh life ideals and sectarian model as its soul and entire Punjab, warring Sikh dominions and all Sikhs its body, but his 'treaty' of 'perpetual friendship' had greatly shattered it. The fettered his feet to lands right to Sutlej restricting his access to Cis-Sutlej states on Sutlej's left. Thus, half of the dream was lost by his indirect acceptance of British supremacy the very spirit of his crusade was deeply eroded.

But despite, Maharaja Ranjit Singh, with his exceptional military genius and great leadership qualities, was able to inspire his Sikhs and extend the territories of Sikh-land deep into the north. This, however, was to a great extent a mere military expansion not very lasting for the lands thus annexed hadn't the ideals of Sikh life embedded into their blood such as had the lands on Sutlej's left. Their annexation was least an emotional merger. The dilemma was obvious. There where political authority craved for promoting Sikh ideals the lands hadn't much of them in their blood, but where they streamed in all vessels the rulers, despite being Sikhs, were indifferent to them, or rather only exploited them for their own political ends. Maharaja Ranjit Singh's efforts were undoubtedly great but they did not bear as great fruits.

Maharaja Ranjit Singh upheld

MAHARAJA RANJIT SINGH WITH HIS NOBLES
Sikh, Punjab, mid 19th century
Paper, 28 x 23.5 cm, Acc. no: 3965
Collection: Govt. Museum and Art Gallery, Chandigarh.

and promoted Sikhism but it was something different which had a deeper impact. Guru Gobind Singh had transformed Nanak's sect into *Khalsa*, a people to ever endure and never perish. Hence, repression more heinous than could be thought of, the ruthless butchering of Banda Bahadur and relentless persecution of thousands of his Sikhs in 1716, failed to eliminate Sikhs' military spirit for it had been enshrined in a people, a nationhood. Maharaja Ranjit Singh alike transformed into 'a soldier' the military spirit of this 'people' of Guru Gobind Singh. Soldier, the individual, was transformed into a cult that ever endured and bred the "bravest and steadiest", had a past of 'brilliant achievenments and grim determinations', and manifested itself in them who fought "with valour of heroes, enthusiasm of crusaders and desperation of zealots sworn to conquer the enemy or die sword in hand."

Hence, when after the death of Maharaja Ranjit Singh in 1839 Sikhs' political authority waned and disintegrated, the Sikh soldier, embodying Sikhs' military spirit, rose and upheld the Sikh cause though every time he was betrayed by self interests of persons in command negotiating against the spirit of *'Panth'*. All battles after Ranjit Singh to include two major Anglo-Sikh wars were most bravely fought by the 'soldier' and as miserbly lost by the treacheries of

MAHARAJA SHER SINGH
Sikh, Punjab, late 19th century
Lithograph after Emily Eden's original drawing
Paper, 55 x 42 cm, Acc. no: 44
Collection: Maharaja Ranjit Singh Museum, Amritsar.

his generals. The failure of 1857 Sepoy Revolt left the Sikh soldier, artisan, worker, peasant in deep anguish, but it also bred in them a stronger feeling of resentment against British colonialism with several minor groups cropping up in defiance. Sikhs' recurring confrontation with British army, non-acceptance of its authority, constant resistance and upsurge against British and a total disquiet prevailing all over Punjab during freedom movement, embodied Sikhs' great 'military spirit', a legacy of the Divine and the reflection of a mortal's dream.

The common Sikh, with a conscience shaped by the teachings of his Gurus and *bani* of Kabir like saints, upheld the flame and let not his resistance die despite often paying heavily for it. The Sikh elite, feudatories, military generals, rich and ecclesiastic posts holders, appeasing the British imperialism by a show of their loyalty, not only acted counterly and shamefully but also derogated the '*Panth*' and strove to extinguish the very flame of *Khalsa*. In 1872 about a hundred Namdharis, a minor organisation of Sikhs deeply devoted to Guru Gobind Singh's ideal of chivalry believing likewise in armed revolution, were ruthlessly gunned for their defiance of the British rule. They were one after other tied on the mouth of tanks and fired, their limbs blown into the air. The Sikh elite,

THE BATTLE OF CHILLIANWALA, THE 2ND ANGLO-SIKH WAR
Sikh, Punjab, dated 13th January 1849
Artist: H.V. Martens, Lithograph engraved by J. Harris
61 x 41 cm, Acc. no: 11
Collection: Maharaja Ranjit Singh Museum, Amritsar.

instead of condemning this heinous act of unprecedented cruelty, passed a resolution approving and appreciating this colonial brutality and their solidarity with the British in India.

Again, on April 13, in 1919, the common masses of Punjab, mostly Sikhs, assembled at Jalianwalla Bagh in Amritsar to voice their disapproval of the newly imposed Rowlatt Acts. Closing all exits they were indiscriminately fired from all sides by machine guns killing, as per British govt.'s own reports, 379 unarmed unprovoked innocent and leaving for dogs to care another 1200 wounded. The cruelty moved the British Parliament and shocked the entire world. But the Sikh elite got up in defence of General Dyer, whose brain had

conceived and hands executed the Jalianwalla Bagh massacre. They not only passed resolutions reaffirming their solidarity with the British but also invited the killer to the Golden Temple and felicitated him with *saropa*, the highest mark of honour in Sikh tradition.

Maharaha Ranjit Singh's dream save what of it reposed in the 'soldier' was thus lost. Most of his feudal successors in Punjab had given up resistance against British imperialism. Sikhs' political authority and military strength had quite weakened. The worst of it was that the affluent Sikh, whatever his area of activity, only countered and eroded what the common one upheld and sustained. He who kept the candle aflame was thus Guru Gobind Singh's 'people'

and Ranjit Singh's dream-child, his 'soldier'. Had it not been the far reaching foresight of Guru Gobind Singh who sought to perpetutate the sect by transforming it into a people and Sikhs' religious authority to the sacred *Granth* from anyone born of flesh and blood, and Maharaja Ranjit Singh's preference for 'soldier' to repose in him his dream, the military spirit of *Khalsa* and the entire Sikh legacy, the Sikh tradition would have been lost in wilderness. Reposed in a soldier's frame, a saint's being, in a common Sikh born with nectar in his throat and the boon of perpetual life, legacy of the 'Divines' and the dream of those who lived to their divine vision is Sikhs' great enduring heritage and a Sikh's life is its mirror.

86

The Divine Inheritance

Adi-Granth: The *Bani* Manifest

THE OPENING FOLIO OF THE *ADI-GRANTH*
Sikh, Punjab, late 19th century, Paper
Collection: National Museum, New Delhi.

The *Adi-granth*, a work of the divine hands, enshrined later as *Panth's* impersonal Guru assuming the name 'Sri Guru Granth Sahib', the holiest in Sikh tradition, had the most profound impact in shaping the 'Sikh', the 'Soldier' and the 'Sikh tradition' and in guiding and inspiring them perpetually. *Sri Guru Granth Sahib* represents the Sikhist vision of the Supreme and embodies at the same time a Sikh's prayer leading his being to salvation, to merge with **Him** in inseparable unity. To a Sikh *Sri Guru Granth Sahib* is the Ultimate incarnate, and in the sacred Book he finds accomplishment of all his aspirations, temporal and transcendental. *Sri Guru Granth Sahib*, the nucleus of Sikh thought and faith, is an entity beyond time incessantly effecting sectarian unity and uniformity of Sikh life. It is capable to so sublimate the perceptional vision in a devotional being that like Kabir's

'Kahun so nam, sunun so sumiran, jo kachhu karun so pooja

he is elevated to a plane where whatever uttered transforms into **His nam**, whatever heard into **His** commemoration and whatever done into **his** worship.

CONSECRATION OF THE *ADI-GRANTH* AT *HARI MANDIR* BY GURU ARJAN
Sikh, Modern, Oil on canvas, Artist: Bodhraj, 1990, 40" x 23"
Collection: Punjab and Sind Bank, New Delhi
Adi-Granth, the collection of the Bani of four earlier Sikh Gurus and of Guru Arjan himself,
and several saints, was installed in full ceremony at new constructed Hari Mandir in Amritsar in 1604.
Baba Buddhaji was nominated the first 'Granthi'.
The painting has highlighted the Guru with nimbus and Baba Buddhaji put in presiding position.

88

At its inception the Sikh *Panth* sprouted with hymns of Guru Nanak or the devotional songs of *Sufis*, Vaishnava saints and poets, which Nanak recited during *sangats*, the congregations where believing minds met for commemorating the Supreme. These songs, endowed with **His** attributes and man's littlenesss and **His** great benefaction and man's humble submission sung first by the Guru and then by the assembly irrespective of whatever Guru's vision or thought of **Him**, his message or prayer, were the earliest manifestations of Sikhism. Such devotional songs, which anyone stored in his mind and recited, low or loud, even during life's routine hubbub, were the vessels that carried the pith far and wide. Guru Nanak was a gifted poet and a born singer. His quest for the Supreme and **His** consequent realisation had enlightened and transformed Nanak into a divine being. Now whatever he uttered was a divine song and its mode the celestial music manifesting his vision of **Him** and his absolute submission. Nanak's vision of **Him** constituted the body of his song, his devotion its spirit and the music that accompanied its breath. Thus a song, endowed with thought, devotion and music came to be Sikh *Panth's* cardinal requisites.

Of the nine personal Sikh Gurus who succeeded Guru Nanak five contributed to the poetic treasure of Sikh *Panth*. Inspired by their Gurus and their teachings some of their *bhaktas*, the followers, too, composed hymns and many of them were sung during *sangats*, the daily congregations. Other devotional songs and hymns that the Sikh Gurus sang during *sangats* belonged to some of the known *Sufis* and Vaishnava saints and Hindu and Muslim poets for in them were as appropriately conveyed their thought, their vision of the divine and soul's yearnings for uniting with the Supreme. This entire poetry, as it has been inherited directly from Gurus, composed and sung, or only sung by them, is revered in Sikh tradition as *Gurbani*. Guru Hargobind, Guru Har Rai and Guru Har Kishan did not add to *Gurbani* any of their own poetry. The poetic works of the Tenth Guru, which have been compiled separately later as the *Dasam-granth*, do not constitute the part of Sri Guru Granth Sahib, though his *Dasam-granth*, too, is held in great reverence.

By the time of the fifth Guru Arjan Sikhism had earned immense popularity with followings all over Punjab. Obviously, dialectic variations, superimpositions, corrupt intonations, pronounciations and linguistic forms, lack of musical discipline and incoherence were found severely affecting the purity of the *Gurbani* and the need of its standardization was greatly felt. Alike, the entire bulk lied scattered in small *pothis*, loose sheets, traders' ledgers, folk tradition, people's memory, bards' and singers' throats, and the need to collect it together was deeply felt. Guru Arjan decided to undertake this two-fold responsibility of compiling and standardizing the entire *Gurbani*, and in the process to set it to appropriate musical modes, the *ragas* and *raginis*.

The task of acquiring *bani-pothis* had its own difficulties for many who had them in their possession were always reluctant to part with them. What prevailed in folk tradition or in mass memory was either very little known or was scattered far and wide usually at remote ends. Teams of collectors and scribes were always on their toes to rush to the spot where a word of *Gurbani* was known to exist. In some more difficult cases, as of Baba Mohanji at Goindwal, Guru Arjan had to himself approach the owners of the *bani-pothis* and persuade them to relinguish the same in *Panth's* larger interests. *Guru Bilas-Chevin Patshahi*, a work of 1718, writes how every time a *pothi*, after it was acquired, was brought to Amritsar in a palanquin in full procession with a crowd of Sikhs following. And many a time Guru Arjan himself walked bare-footed behind it and his son and successor Guru

ਤੇਰੇ ਗਰਿਖ ਰਾਖੁ ਵਡ ਵਡੇ ਹੋ ਜਨ ਨਾਨਕ ਨਾਮੁ ਅਧਾਰ ਟੇਕ ਹੈ ਹਰਿ ਨਾਮੇ ਹੀ ਸੁਖ ਮੇਰਾ ਹੋ ॥੪॥ ਰਾਗੁ ਗਉੜੀ ਪੂਰਬੀ ਮਹਲਾ ੫ ॥ ਕਰਉ ਬੇਨੰਤੀ ਸੁਣਹੁ ਮੇਰੇ ਮੀਤ ਸੰਤ ਟਹਲ ਕੀ ਬੇਲਾ ॥ ਈਹਾ ਖਾਟਿ ਚਲਹੁ ਹਰਿ ਲਾਹਾ ਆਗੈ ਬਸਨੁ ਸੁਹੇਲਾ ॥੧॥ ਅਉਧ ਘਟੈ ਦਿਨਸੁ ਰੈਣਾਰੇ ॥ ਮਨ ਗੁਰ ਮਿਲਿ ਕਾਜ ਸਵਾਰੇ ॥੧॥ ਰਹਾਉ ॥ ਇਹੁ ਸੰਸਾਰੁ ਬਿਕਾਰੁ ਸੰਸੇ ਮਹਿ ਤਰਿਓ ਬ੍ਰਹਮ ਗਿਆਨੀ ॥ ਜਿਸਹਿ ਜਗਾਇ ਪੀਆਵੈ ਇਹੁ ਰਸੁ ਅਕਥ ਕਥਾ ਤਿਨਿ ਜਾਨੀ ॥ ਜਾ ਕਉ ਆਏ ਸੋਈ ਬਿਹਾਝਹੁ ਹਰਿ ਗੁਰ ਤੇ ਮਨਹਿ ਬਸੇਰਾ ॥ ਨਿਜ ਘਰਿ ਮਹਲੁ ਪਾਵਹੁ ਸੁਖ ਸਹਜੇ ਬਹੁਰਿ ਨ ਹੋਇਗੋ ਫੇਰਾ ॥੩॥ ਅੰਤਰਜਾਮੀ ਪੁਰਖ ਬਿਧਾਤੇ ਸਰਧਾ ਮਨ ਕੀ ਪੂਰੇ ॥ ਨਾਨਕ ਦਾਸੁ ਇਹੈ ਸੁਖੁ ਮਾਗੈ ਮੋ ਕਉ ਕਰਿ ਸੰਤਨ ਕੀ ਧੂਰੇ ॥੪॥੧॥

ਸਿਰੀਰਾਗੁ ਮਹਲਾ ੧ ਪਹਿਲਾ ॥ ਘਰੁ ੧ ॥

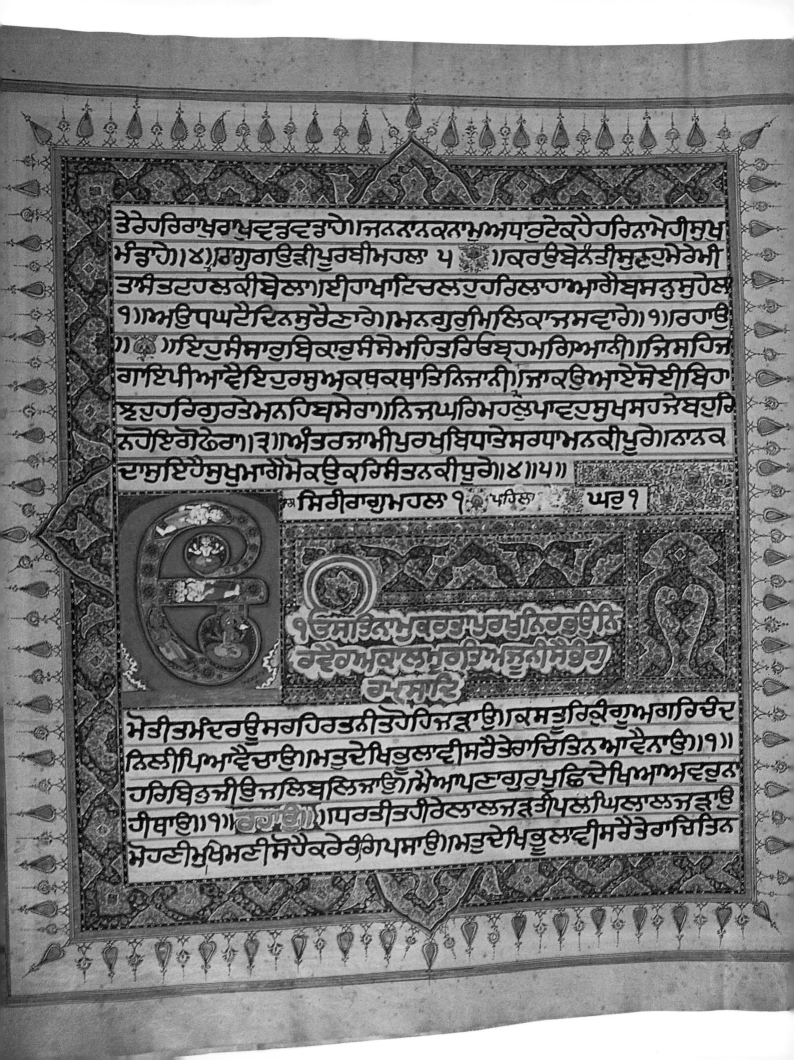

ੴ ਸਤਿ ਨਾਮੁ ਕਰਤਾ ਪੁਰਖੁ ਨਿਰਭਉ ਨਿਰਵੈਰੁ ਅਕਾਲ ਮੂਰਤਿ ਅਜੂਨੀ ਸੈਭੰ ਗੁਰ ਪ੍ਰਸਾਦਿ ॥

ਮੋਤੀ ਤ ਮੰਦਰ ਊਸਰਹਿ ਰਤਨੀ ਤ ਹੋਹਿ ਜੜਾਉ ॥ ਕਸਤੂਰਿ ਕੁੰਗੂ ਅਗਰਿ ਚੰਦਨਿ ਲੀਪਿ ਆਵੈ ਚਾਉ ॥ ਮਤੁ ਦੇਖਿ ਭੂਲਾ ਵੀਸਰੈ ਤੇਰਾ ਚਿਤਿ ਨ ਆਵੈ ਨਾਉ ॥੧॥ ਹਰਿ ਬਿਨੁ ਜੀਉ ਜਲਿ ਬਲਿ ਜਾਉ ॥ ਮੈ ਆਪਣਾ ਗੁਰੁ ਪੂਛਿ ਦੇਖਿਆ ਅਵਰੁ ਨਾਹੀ ਥਾਉ ॥੧॥ ਰਹਾਉ ॥ ਧਰਤੀ ਤ ਹੀਰੇ ਲਾਲ ਜੜਤੀ ਪਲਘਿ ਲਾਲ ਜੜਾਉ ॥ ਮੋਹਣੀ ਮੁਖਿ ਮਣੀ ਸੋਹੈ ਕਰੇ ਰੰਗਿ ਪਸਾਉ ॥ ਮਤੁ ਦੇਖਿ ਭੂਲਾ ਵੀਸਰੈ ਤੇਰਾ ਚਿਤਿ ਨ

Hargobind receiving them with band of musicians and singers on the outskirts of the city.

The material so acquired was usually placed to the custody of Mata Ganga, Guru's spouse, before Guru Arjan undertook to scrutinize and give dictation of its final version to Bhai Gurdas who with a fine hand served as scribe. In the process of scrutiny, the fake and superimposed was deleted, genuine retained, structural errors and linguistic variations and corruptions weeded out and purity of language, correctness of theme and the pith of each verse rigorously re-discovered. It was a threefold job involving rectification of errors, protection of the *bani* from the grabbling of schismatic bands and its preservation for the posterity. The script the *bani* was complied in was *Gurmukhi*, but the languages used originally by poets and saints were retained. The local dialect by Sikh Gurus, and Persian, Urdu, Sanskrit, Brijbhasha etc. used by others represented a multi-lingual character of the Holy *Granth*. The overtunes of Islam, Vaishnavism and *Sufism* flavouring these hymns and poetic expressions were carefully retained. This collection of *bani* was the 'Adi-granth'. The inscription of Bhai Gurdas on the top of its index page reads— 'Sambat 1661 miti bhadon vadi ekam pothi likhi pahuche', that is, the *Granth* was completed by

August 1604. After its completion the holy Book was installed on a high-raised *vedika*, the pedestal, in the central hall of Hari Mandir during following year's Diwali congregation in full ceremony and with great veneration.

Guru Arjan was a fine singer and instrumentalist. He hence knew that a text unless reproduced effectively left poor impact, where as it could deeply move, sublimate and elevate a listener's emotions and vision if produced with effective musical discipline, proper intonations and placing of words. He hence did not leave the *bani* as a mere textual thing but rather set most of it to the musical discipline of *ragas* and *raginis*. Each verse or hymn was so placed that its words fell on the important notes of its concerned *raga-raginis*, effected deeper sublimation and greater intellectual elevation. It was thus that the *Adi-granth* had from its very inception music as its essence, a music which brims with irresistible mystique and is so full of surprises. Guru Arjan used 31 main *ragas* and *raginis*, though the basis of such classification, restricting their number to just 31, is somewhat difficult to discern for their approved number in Indian classics is different. He also used 30 mixed *raga*-forms usually prevailing in Indian classical singing.

A part of *bani*, usually consisting of *varan*, 22 in all, was left to

be sung as the folk tradition demanded. Only nine of these 22 *varan*, composed in ballad-form, had prescibed modes of singing. Guru Arjan, by mixing together the forms of Vaishnava *bhajan* and Islamic *kufi*, created a kind of catholicity of the style of *Adi-granth's* music and while searching new ways to effect spiritual elevation of his Sikhs he discovered many new effects and possibilites contained in *ragas* and classical singing.

The first copy scribed by Bhai Gurdas, complete with index and affixed with Guru Arjan's seal of authority, contained in its 974 leaves of 12" x 8" size. It comprises of the poetry of Guru Nanak, Guru Angad, Guru Amardas, Guru Ramdas and Guru Arjan, fifteen Vaishnava and *Sufi* saints and poets and a few *varan* and verses of four minstrels. The compositions, known as *sabads* in Sikh tradition, were arranged in order of the succession of the Gurus and the verses of *bhaktas* were included thereafter in the same *raga*-format. The entire Holy *Granth* was paginated and its index was prepared with the opening words of each *sabad*, something evidencing great methodicity and a high degree of organizational skill.

To the *Adi-granth* were later added 116 *sabads* of the nineth Guru Teg Bahadur by his son Guru Gobind Singh before he reposed

91

with the holy Book the Guruship of the *Panth*. The revised copy of the *Granth* by the Tenth Guru contained 1430 pages. After the earlier copy he had prepared at Paonta was lost when he crossed river Sarsa he prepared, it is said, its new copy out of his memory by dictating to Bhai Mani Singh all its 1430 pages. *Sri Guru Granth Sahib* came to be *Panth's* deity incarnate, immortal and beyond time, as also beyond decay or change after it was deified, consecrated and venerated as the Guru of the *Panth*. Hence, ever after its number of pages and form remained unchanged. Now its standard printed copies too contain 1430 pages, 5900 *sabads* or hymns and 15575 stanzas, which include 974 *sabads* of Guru Nanak, 62 of Guru Angad, 907 of Guru Amardas, 679 of Guru Ramdas and 2218 of Guru Arjan, and 922 *sabads* of the 15 Vaishnava and *Sufi* saints and poets, namely, Kabir, Namdeva, Ravidas, Baba Farid, Dhanna, Bhikha, Beni, Trilochan, Jaidev, Surdas, Sadna, Sen, Ramananda, Parmanand and Pipa. The four minstrels are Mardana, Satta, Balwand and Sundar. Faith, philosophy and music, and their subordinate organs, the ethical values, community life, poetic excellences, humanism and love, constitute the very being, the body and the soul, of the *Sri Guru Granth Sahib*.

THE OPENING PAGE OF THE *ADI-GRANTH* WITH THE '*MOOL MANTRA*'
IN GURU TEG BAHADUR'S OWN HAND
Sikh, Punjab, dated A.D. 1666, Script: Gurmukhi
Paper, Folios: 579, Acc. no: M/341
Collection: Patiala Archives, Patiala.

Illuminated copies of Sri Guru Granth Sahib

THE COSMIC LOTUS: a folio of *Sri Guru Granth Sahib*
Sikh–Kashmiri mix style, dated A.D.1839
Paper, 44.5 x 44 cm, Acc. no.: 59.155/2
Collection: National Museum, New Delhi
*This folio of Sri Guru Granth Sahib conceives the universe as divided into twelve petals
of a lotus representing twelve zodiac divisions. Ten of these petals illustrate the ten Sikh Gurus
and the other two their origin. The centre of the lotus has inside it Sodhi Bhan Singh,
obviously the patron who got this manuscript prepared, worshipping Mahakala.*

Initially, a copy of the *Adi-granth* with plain text and no illustrations was more favoured. The preference however seems to have shifted from plain to illuminated borders in Quranic fashion, within 50-60 years after the *granth* came into being, which its copy dated 1666 available with Patiala Archives clearly suggests. This copy has some illuminated folios and the prefacing one inscribed on it the *Mul-Mantra* in Guru Teg Bahadur's own hand. A number of such illuminated copies of the *Adi-granth* from 18th and 19th centuries, mostly revised as *Sri Guru Granth Sahib*, have been reported by various sources.

The National Museum, New Delhi, too has in its collection a number of illuminated copies of the holy Book. More important, however, is the existence of the holy *Granth's* two illustrated copies in its collection for the cult of illustrating *Sri Guru Granth Sahib* was not much in preference. The existence of these copies indicates that the tradition of illustrating the sacred Book, howsoever scanty, had come to prevail by late 18th century which is the approximate period of these copies. They are extensively illustrated. One of these copies is smaller in size whereas the other one is larger with 52 x 54.5 cm folio size and a dated one of 1839.

This highly expensive and hence ambitious large size copy of the Holy *Granth* seems to have been prepared for some Sodhi

Bhan Singh portrayed worshipping divinities in one of its prefacing folios. The date of the completion of this copy of the holy Book coincides with the date of Maharaja Ranjit Singh's death. One of its folio records:

Samvat 1896 var sudi purnima Ranjit Singh sakha joti jot samane

Obviously, it is either Sodhi Bhan Singh's dedication of the Holy *Granth* to the memory of Maharaja Ranjit Singh or he got this copy prepared for gifting it to the great champion of the Sikh *Panth*. A similar copy, with its prefacing folios illustrated alike, though the later ones left incomplete only with line drawings, is in the possession of former *jagir*

of Bagariyan now in Nabha, Punjab. It suggests that after he decided to gift the first copy to Maharaja Ranjit Singh, Sodhi Bhan Singh went for acquiring another similar copy for himself. In 1959, the National Museum, New Delhi, was able to acquire five of its illustrated loose folios but in 1961 the entire copy of the holy Book reached its collection.

One of these folios depicts the zodiac with its twelve astronomical divisions represented here by a twelve petalled lotus, the ten painted with the figures of Ten Gurus with their families, and the other two their Surya and Chandra *vanshi* origin. The circle created in the centre by the circumference of the petals contains the figure of its patron Sodhi Bhan Singh

worshipping Mahakala and Goddess Kali, may be Sodhi Bhan Singh was a Shaiva but no less devoted to canons of Sikh Gurus. Two others depict 31 *ragas* and *raginis*, an essential and integral part of *Gurbani* and one of Sikhs' sacred institutions. A fourth one depicts *Vishwa-rupa*, the cosmic form of Krishna, a concept parallel to Sikhs' concept of the *Akal*

THE OPENING PAGE OF ILLUMINATED MANUSCRIPT OF SRI GURU GRANTH SAHIB
Sikh, Punjab, early 19th century
Paper, 22 x 24 cm, Script: Gurmukhi
Acc. no: 61.356
Collection: National Museum, New Delhi
This manuscript consists of 673 folios of which 40 are illuminated
It is in finely calligraphed Gurmukhi characters.

Karta Purukh, the All-doing, All-creating Timeless One Who reveals in all forms, pervades them all and creates them all from within **His** own Being and is thus the Proto-form.

Fifth and sixth folios seem to depict themes, which are somewhat Vaishnavite, one (unpublished) depicting the three tiered cosmos consisting of the Vishnu, Brahma, and *Indraloka* and the other various *Vaishnava* deities with Vishnu presiding. In an arrangement similar to the earlier one the zodiac has been divided by a twelve petalled lotus, each containing on it one *Vaishnava* god, the circle created by their circumference the *Sheshshayi* Vishnu attended by Lakshmi and Brahma riding the lotus rising from his navel and the framing space on its all four sides the 24 incarnations of Vishnu. These two folios little collate with the Sikh thought and might be the part of an art tradition, or an essentiality of artist's conditioned mind, seeking to scribe a prayer-text but not without the sacred images prefacing such text.

The essence of Sikhism, thus, lies in *bani* for it is in *bani* that **He** reveals **Himself**. *Sangeet*, the music, is the flavour of the *Gurbani*, nectaral, sublimating and elevational, and thought, devotion and dedication are its pith. In Sikhism *Bani* is essentially transcendental for the moment it is born, it transforms the entire being. It sublimates emotions and elevates the intellect, and the sublimation of emotions leads to the realm of spiritualism, absolute union and eternal joy, and the elevation of intellect to the realm of thought where entire cosmos reveals itself to the thinking mind. Thus, after **He** is known and the dedication to **Him** becomes absolute in an inseperable union the being steps into eternal joy which he himself is and knows all for he is now the all knowing Mind, the cosmos manifest. Thus *bani* has its three inherent components- the music that sublimates and is its flavour, the devotion that gives it its purpose, and the thought that gives it its meaning. In Sikhism *Gurmat* encompasses all that relates to thought and devotion and *Gurmat Sangeet* all that disciplines and add flavour to *bani*.

SHESHSAYI VISHNU AND HIS TEN INCARNATIONS
Sikh–Kashmiri mix style, dated A.D. 1839
Paper, 44.5 x 44 cm, Acc. no: 59.155/3
Collection: National Museum, New Delhi
This folio of Sri Guru Granth Sahib depicts Sheshsayi Vishnu
along his ten incarnations on lotus petals representing
cosmos as does the cosmic lotus.

A FOLIO OF SRI GURU GRANTH SAHIB DEPICTING BRAHMA, VISHNU AND *INDRA LOKAS*
Sikh–Kashmiri mix style, dated A.D. 1839
Paper, 52.5 x 47 cm, Acc.no: 59.526
Collection: National Museum, New Delhi.
*This third folio of the same large size manuscript of Sri Guru Granth Sahib depicts three planes
of cosmic existence as have been conceived in Hindu mythology, though the Sikh ideology
little agreed with any such thing. May be, the artist was led by the tradition of rendering religious
texts but with such broad, wide and holy beginning.*

Gurmat Sangeet

◆

THE RECITATION OF SRI GURU GRANTH SAHIB
Sikh, Punjab, dated June 1858 A.D.
Artist: William Carpenter, Paper, 34.5 x 24 cm
Collection: Hotel Imperial, New Delhi.

(Opposite page bottom) BEBE NANAKI PRESENTING *RABBAB* TO BHAI MARDANA
Sikh, Punjab, Modern, Oil on canvas, 27" x 24"
Artist: Bodhraj, 1976
Collection: Punjab and Sind Bank, New Delhi.

THE FOLIO OF SRI GURU GRANTH SAHIB DEPICTING *RAGAS-RAGINIS*
Sikh–Kashmiri mix style, dated A.D. 1839
Paper, 44.5 x 44 cm, Acc. no: 59.525
Collection: National Museum, New Delhi.

The Sikh Panth is basically the way of realizing Him in devotion, commemoration and singing of His Nam being its best modes. The music has, thus, in Sikh Panth a place as high as Gurmat or Gurbani and gets for it the name Gurmat sangeet, the sacred Sikh music. Here this folio divided in eighteen compartments has in each of them one traditional symbolic representation of one of the ragas or raginis, the various modes of Indian classical music.

All Sikh Gurus are known to blend music with *bani* when communicating themselves to masses, though under strict discipline imposed by various *ragas-raginis*. After Guru Arjan had compiled Gurus' *bani* and set it to the discipline of various *ragas-raginis* music came to be considered as an integral part of the *bani* itself. Acquiring for itself the name *Gurmat Sangeet* and elevated to same level as *Gurbani* or *Gurmat* the music became in Sikh *Panth* an institution as venerated as *bani* itself. And, after the *Adi-granth* had been installed in Hari Mandir and *ragis* and *rabbabis* required to adhere to musical prescription, when reproducing *Gurbani*, the *Gurmat Sangeet* was defined.

Instead of ensnaring a being into the cobweb of any metaphysics the Sikh Gurus sought the soul's liberation from the material bonds along a devotional line in the soul's unity with the Supreme attainable by just *simaran* of his **Nam.** They little preached even against the fallacies of this material world or anything like a philosophy. They only discovered a path leading to **Him** by commemorating **His** name which helped realise **Him** within one's own being and considered music, a song sung in **His** devotion, with its form and spirit sublimated by formative discipline and spiritual flavour to produce required effect, as the best mode of such realisation.

Music served two ends, sensual and spiritual; hence, by tying it under strict sanctity norms and discipline *ragas* and *raginis*, the Sikh Gurus transformed it into the most potent vessel of sublimating emotions and elevating intellect and thereby rise to **His** vision leaving the material plane below. Music, now shaped by Gurus to a commanded form and for giving the required result and is hence *Gurmat sangeet*, is thus as much a part of Sikh *Panth* as *Gurmat* or *Gurbani* and as great a legacy.

Gurmat

Gurmat, the Sikh thought, is a quest for total life, now and hereafter. It relates to individual living, in relation to his material fold, society, nation, community of man, one's own being and in relation to others. It seeks to discover truth, the true One, the transcendental Supreme and the ways leading to **His** realisation and soul's union with **Him**. It discovers means of liberation, attainment of supreme bliss and eternal joy and condenses into a syllable the mystery of the cosmos.

Good individual living is the essence of *Gurmat* for it leads to universal goodness, promotes casteless-creedless love, fraternity, equality, tolerance, peace and harmony and breeds in man qualities of austerity, abstinence, freedom from enmity, ill-will and vengeance, forgiveness, compassion, purity. It builds instrinsic strength and bears good-will to all. *Gurmat* insists for complete detachment arrived at by eradicating ego, holding on truth and for preserving the *gurmat* a willingness for any kind of sacrifice, unresisting and non-violent. It demands resoluteness, steadfastness, dauntless courage and resistance against all oppressions. It embodies in such sainthood wherein good is returned for evil, none is known as enemy, hands rise only to bless, man is seen in his impersonal role and

BABA NANAK WEARING *CHOGA*
INSCRIBED WITH JAPUJI IN *GURMUKHI* SCRIPT
Sikh, Punjab, 20th century
Collection: Punjab Archives, Patiala.

100

authority reposes in institution. It believes the good individual is the foundation of a good society, better and stronger nation, a great world and an excellent manhood.

Gurmat does not approve renunciation for one may discover within one's material fold means of spiritual upliftment leading to the soul's communion with the Supreme and to the attainment of eternal bliss. Purity is the essence of all thought but to abide pure amidst impurities of the material life is the crux of *Gurmat*. It rather prescribes *sangat*, a mode for seeking and realizing **Him** conjointly, for by meeting, feeding, praying and communicating together, besides **His** realisation, one knows mankind better and the ties of mutual love, self-restraint and self-discipline get stronger. Pathos, a feeling different from worldly unhappiness, and the inner bliss, something different from material happiness, are seen in *Gurmat* as index to soul's restlessness, particularly when it yearns to unite with the Supreme.

Japu ji contemplates **Him** as *Ek- Omkar, Nirankar, Sat, Karta, Akal, Saibhang, Purkh*, that is, there is but one God. He is Formless, True, All-doing, All creating, Timeless, Unborn and Imperishable, or never born yet ever existing. **He** does not know vengeance, hatred, ego and the like and is beyond time and pervades the Universe. **He** is not born, nor dies to be born again. **He** is self-existent and existed before anything came into being and shall persist after all things perish. **He** is *Nirankar*, the Formless, yet precedes all forms. **He** is *Sat*, the True, for all things, save **Him**, decay, change and perish. **He** manifests in cosmos, and *bani*, a concept likethat of Vedic *Vak-Shakti*, is the most potent instrument of **His** realization. **He** is beyond fear, enmity and all passions, and is both immanent and transcendental. The personalness of Hindu God, the spiritual equality of Buddhism and the congregation of Islam seem to have combined in Sikh concept of **Him**.

In *Gurmat Nam simaran* is the purest and most effective form of **His** worship. *Nam simaran* introverts the vision from without to within where **He** is always present. By Guru's grace alone **His** worship is accomplished. One who leads a pure and detached life and has forsaken ego is able to realize **Him** in worship which is best expressed in *sarvan, pad-sevana, archana, vandana, das-bhav, maitri-bhava and atma-nivedana*, that is, in listening to **His Nam**, worshipping **His** feet, making offerings, praying, submitting, serving friend-like and eradicating ego.

101

SIMARINI OR ROSARY OF GURU HARGOBIND
Collection: Bhai Rattan Singh of Daroli Bhai, Moga, Punjab
Simarani, being the prime vehicle of 'Nam' Simran and His realization, has great sanctity and significance in Sikhism. All Gurus from Baba Nanak to the Tenth Guru had Simarini as essential part of their being. This sacred relic is claimed to have once belonged to Guru Hargobind.

Langar or Guru ka langar

◆

In Sikh tradition most of its values have been attained in practices rather than in preaching and this began in Sikhism with *langar*, the earliest and the most effective of all its institutions, the other one, as much effective though not as much early, being *sangat*. *Langar* gave to Sikhism most of its social values and its humanism and *sangat* effected spiritual elevation through devotion and guided the self to liberation.

Once, Guru Nanak's father gave Nanak some money for starting his own businesss with instructions to strike with it some good bargain, *Khara sauda*, which profitted him. On his way to market Nanak met some *sadhus* who had not eaten anything for past many days. Nanak bought with the money his father had given him for *Khara sauda* some eatables and feasted the *sadhus* and himself sitting together. It was probably in this incident of Nanak's life that the seeds of *langar* concept lied. When back, his father asked him of his bargain and gain. Nanak coolly said, he struck the *Sachcha sauda*, a truer bargain, instead, to reap out of it far greater gains. This incident was not only a pre-runner of *langar* but also Nanak's first step towards his Enlightenment.

Langar, a Persian word meaning an almshouse, was in great prevalence with *Sufis* during 12th -13th centuries. Guru Nanak, sharing many things with *Sufis*, might have taken the *Langar* concept from them in his practices, though in the hands of Sikh Gurus it came to be a far more effective and subtle instrument of many social reforms and added with spiritual sanctity, one of Sikhs' most important institutions. By promoting community feasting with no distinction whatsoever Sikh Gurus sought to equalize all beyond caste, creed, race, religion or social status and mobilised voluntary cooperation to widen later to *kar-sewa*. In Sikhism *langar* has priority over even *sangat* for it eradicated all barriers of material world and unless these were eradicated how would the process of soul's liberation begin.

Mata Khiwi distributing *Kheer* to *Sangat*
Sikh, Punjab, Modern, 1980, Oil on canvas
Artist: Devender Singh
Collection: Punjab and Sind Bank, New Delhi.
The Sikh institution of Langar was imparted further sanctity by Mata Kiwi who herself prepared Langar and fed the sangat by her own hands. And, it is for her such contribution that Sri Guru Granth Sahib commemorates her, the only lady to have such honour 'Balwand Kiwi nekjan jis bahuti chhau pratrayi, langar daulat wandian rasa amrit khir ghilayi'.

LORD VISHNU'S INCARNATIONS
folio from the *Dasam Granth*
Sikh, Punjab, circa A.D. 1860-70, Paper
This folio depicts in the traditional way Kurma and Matsyavatara
(tortoise and fish), two of lord Vishnu's incarnations.

Dasam-granth, the Book of the Tenth, another important document of Sikhs, is the name of the collected works of the Tenth Sikh Guru. It represents a different temperament of Sikh community and in its theme, spirit and object marks a departure from the writings of prior Sikh Gurus. *Dasam-granth* manifests Guru Gobind Singh's great poetic genius and his resoluteness striving to foster in Sikhs the spirit of self-confidence, self reliance, chivalry and sacrifice and his effort to draw from past and from others' religious traditions strength and inspiration for present. The *Granth* embodies a Sikh's incessant battle against ills, wrongs, oppression and reflects the eternal conflict between good and evil.

Dasam-granth, comprising initially of his *Jap Sahib, Chandi-di-var, Chandi Charita, Gian Prabodh, Chaubis-avatara, Rama-avatara, Brahma-avatara, Rudra-avatara, Bichitra-Natak, Akal Ustat* and random *sawaiyas, shlokas* and *chaupais*, was compiled by his old devotee Bhai Mani Singh some 20 years after Guru's death at the instance of his consort Mata Sunderi. In Guru Gobind Singh's life-time Bhai Mani Singh had scribed *Sri Guru Granth Sahib* dictated by him. When Guru Gobind Singh evacuated Anandpur Sahib in 1705 most of his works were lost

104

and thus Bhai Mani Singh's job was rendered more difficult taking him years to collect his material scattered here and there and prepare the desired copy. Later in 1885 *Gurmat Granth Pracharak Sabha* undertook to prepare a more accomplished copy of Guru's works. The *Sabha* collected from different sources 32 copies of the *Granth* and got the entire material scrutinized by a body of scholars. Later in 1902, the *Sabha* published the final copy of the *Granth*.

Guru Gobind Singh believed and promoted faith in One Formless, yet in his writings recourse to Hindu *Puranic* themes and deities is as much evident. The reason seems obvious. The cir-

(Previous page) A FOLIO FROM *DASAM-GRANTH*
Sikh, Punjab, circa A.D. 1860-70
Paper, 39 x 36 cm, Acc. no.: 94.13
Collection: National Museum, New Delhi
The compilation of the poetic works of the Tenth Guru. This manuscript of
the Dasam-Granth consists of 736 folios of which 40 are illustrated.

cumstances he chose to fall in required him to be a soldier first. His disciples were all Sikhs but not all his soldiers. Besides, when in process of composing this bulk, all hill chiefs stood united against him in war as well in mispropagation spreading discontentment amongst his soldiers alleging him as anti-Hindu. Such state of mind explains his recourse to Vaishanava themes for he could not otherwise undo this mischievous propagand, motivate his people and win their confidence. Besides, as to Kabir his Rama was not Ayodhya's prince or Dasharath's son but the formless, timeless, all pervading One, so to Guru Gobind Singh *Chandi*, different from a deity, symbolised 'sword', power and ultimately *Akal*, the timeless One. It was apparently his vision of other deities.

Guru Gobind Singh also knew that these Puranic myths had great motivational potentials. His *Var Sri Bhagautiji ki*, a ballad depicting Goddess Chandi crusading against Mahishasura and other demons and thus allegorizing the eternal conflict between good and evil, encouraged soldiers to stand against all that was unjust, cruel and oppressive, and to adhere to righteousness. The warlike temper of the ballad was more relevant to Guru Gobind Singh's purpose. *Chandi Charita*, a composition in *Brajbhasha* depicting her exploits, was aimed at creating amongst

his people a spirit of chivalry and individual dignity. It is divided in 8 cantos and comprises of 233 couplets. Guru Gobind Singh's absorption with his theme is so deeply felt that artists illustrating later the copies of the *Dasam-Granth* painted Guru Gobind Singh standing with his hands folded in *Devi's* worship.

Gian Prabodh, the enlightened knowledge, and *Akal Ustat*, in praise of the Timeless, are works of philosophical profundity. *Gian Prabodh*, a work in *Brajbhasha*, elaborates in its first part the vision of Almighty who is supreme, infinite, invisible and beyond comprehension, desire and fear. The second part, illustrating the stories from *Mahabharata* like those of Parikshat, Janamejaya and his son, is a practical vision of the world. The central theme of *Akal Ustat*, in *Brajbhasha* and *Gurmukhi* character with 271 verses, is the same Timeless, Eternal One, who is Omnipotent, Creator and Sustainer of the universe. It concludes with hope of universal brotherhood as man, wherever he was, sought and praised only one God, a thread that tied all together. *Bichitra Natak*, his biography, first invokes *Bhagauti*, the embodiment of the divine principle crusading for justice and then his predecessors. When recalling his father Guru Teg Bahadur "who sacrificed his life to save the symbols of Hinduism, a deed unparalleled

for heroism in the Kaliyuga", he is swept by emotions. In sixth canto he begins of himself, "*Ab apani katha bakhanon*", acclaiming the object of his life,"*Ham ehi kaj jagat maun aye, dharam het gurudev pathaye*". The cantos from 7 to 13 deals with hill-chiefs' recurring attacks and details of ensuing battles. *Bichitra Natak* is

(Above) DURGA SLAYING DEMONS
A folio of *Dasam Granth*.
Though not much in agreement with Sikh traditions, Guru Gobind Singh wrote in praise of Devi Bhagvati, obviously for inspring his soldiers, for she was traditionally worshipped as a Goddess of war and incarnation of Shakti.

(Below) SURYA-THE SUN GOD
A folio of *Dasam Granth*.

a bold and open statement of God's will and Guru Gobind Singh's role in the world.

These poetic works are endowed with great literary merit. Though composed with a purpose in mind and by the propounder of a *Panth* for the appreciation of their merit they beseech not any sectarian favour. Allegories, similes and symbolism used in them are very powerful and accurate. The use of similes in a succession to arrive at the desired temper is quite interesting. Further effects are created by adding to it dignified and echoic music of the richest timbre. His diction and style, a blend of devotion, lyricism and philosophical serenity, is simply unique. A rich variety of poetic forms and metres marks his works. He sang of God, righteousness, wars and crusades, India's glorious past, gods and goddesses, lovers and martyrs and a large variety of other themes. He embodied the philosophy of light and religion of love and bequeathed to mankind a rarer legacy of literature, thought, emotions and history.

It is significant that as early as 1885 *Gurmat Granth Pracharak Sabha*, seeking to prepare a more accomplished copy of the *Dasam-granth*, was able to acquire its 32 copies, an indication that after Bhai Mani Singh's first copy dateable circa 1730 to 1885 a good number of its copies had been prepared. Illumination and illus-

tration were the high marks of text-calligraphy during the corresponding period. As such the copies of *Dasam-granth* would not have been without illustration or illumination.

The National Museum, New Delhi has in its collection an excellent illustrated copy of the *Dasam-granth* dateable 1860-70, preceding its first published copy by some 50 years. The Pahari touches in illustration and *Gurmukhi* calligraphy suggest that the unknown artist of this manuscript was some Pahari painter migrated to Punjab. The works included in the manuscript are *Jap Sahib, Chandi-di-var, Chandi Charit, Gian Prabodh, Chaubis Avatara, Rama Avatara, Brahma Avatara, Rudravatara, Bichitra Natak and Akal Ustat*, and a few *sawaiyas, slokas* and *chaupais*.

Its first two pages have on their corners eight paintings. The top left is painted with syllable Om superimposed with figures of Vishnu, Brahma and Shiva. The lower left corner has seated on a lotus figure of Ganesh, his consort and a lady offering him *modakas*. The top-right is Goddess Chandi standing on a corpse and a figure suggestive of Guru Gobind Singh standing in devotion. Below right is goddess Saraswati seated on her swan. A serpent around her neck is a quaint addition. A finely decorated bordered circle in the centre of the

page has 12 lines of *Jap Sahib* calligraphed neatly with black, red and gold.

In a similar arrangement the second page has respectively ten-armed *panch-mukhi Svachhanda Bhairava* Shiva with Parvati and a devotee, Goddess Chandi emerging from Agni, the fire, and a devotee-warrior standing before her with body armour on his person, Guru Nanak seated under a tree and his constant companions Bala and Mardana, and Guru Gobind Singh riding a white horse with four followers and a *chhatra*-holder. He is carrying a white falcon, shield and sword. In border decoration Mughal and Kashmiri elements dominate.

The manuscript has forty more illustrations depicting mainly goddess Durga alongwith other *devis* fighting out demons, *Narsimha avatara, Chandravatara, Kalki, Surya, Brahma, Krishnavatara,* along with *Buddhavatra* of Vishnu, *Rudravatra*, Parshuram and *Vamanavatara*, Nara-Narayana, Janmeyajay *yajna* and a few other *Puranic* themes. An interesting departure from the earlier tradition is seen in portrayal of Devi seated on a Company style chair instead a Pahari throne and the gods around in worship. All illustrations are painted with text neatly manuscribed in black and red, and gold used for emphasis and beauty. The purity of the surface has been maintained.

Zafar Namah

◆

Zafar-Namah, an excellent piece of poetry, is a letter written to Mughal emperor Aurangzeb in the year 1706, just a year before his death, by Guru Gobind Singh from Dina Kangarh, a small village in Faridkot district, where he was able to gain some respite from his strenuous wandering of about a year after he had evacuated Anandpur Sahib. The news of the execution of his two infant sons by the Nawab of Sirhind had emotionally moved him and provoked to write this letter. *Zafar-Namah*, meaning a victory message, was Guru Gobind Singh's acclamation of victory over the Mughal emperor for despite that the Mughal emperor inflicted on him most inhuman and heinous atrocities he could not subdue his spirits and kill his resistance.

Zafar-Namah is a long narrative poem consisting of 111 stanzas. The script of the poem is Persian and its form a metered verse. *Zafar-Namah* was carried to Aurangzeb at Ahmednagar where he was camping by two of Guruji's followers, Bhai Daya Singh and Bhai Dharam Singh. Initially the *Zafar-Namah* was not included in *Dasam-granth* when Bhai Mani Singh compiled it, a practice which sustained for long, though now it is very much the part of *Dasam-granth*.

Zafar-Namah, though not by its length, chapterization or other formative disciplines, is the epic of Guru Gobind Singh's life in the same way as was Hemingway's novel 'The oldman and the Sea' where smile wins but only to dip into deeper pathos, the victory is gained but exploits of the victory do not reach the victorious hands. Materially Guru Gobind Singh had lost all but spiritually God's kingdom was his own. This sublimity of his divine pathos, being the cental theme of *Zafar-Namah*, transforms the poem into the epic of life. And it seems Guru Gobind Singh meant to make it so, for he gave it the epic-like metre and preamble affirming his faith in the Almighty. It is not so much the theme as is the vein of pathos that binds and elevates the narrative of the *Zafar-Namah* to a height corresponding to an epic.

Zafar-Namah, despite that it was written with a pathetic mind, manifests an exalted mood and great spiritual fervour. It condemns the unjust and the cruel and hails the true and morally correct. Alleging the emperor of heinous atrocities on innocent, committed by him or his functionaries, he reminds that a sovereign had to be as absolutely truthful and just as an ordinary citizen. And, he said, when all doors to justice and truth are closed, there is every justification for unsheathing the sword: "*Chu kar as Hama hilate dar guzasht, halal ast*

burdan ba shamshir dost"

A 1872 manuscript scribed by Raja Ram Kaul Tota, the son of Pandit Ram Tota, both the illustrious courtiers of Maharaja Ranjit Singh's court, has been reported from Patiala Archives. It contains 60 folios, 58 with text and 2 illustrated. Its first part contains the account of Guru Nanak's visit to Mecca and his hymns composed in *raga Tilang*. Its second part consists of *Zafar-Namah*. Its script is Persian, the same as was originally used by Guru Gobind Singh. Though the manuscript has only two illustrated folios, yet the use of exceptionally thick and fine coloured paper and neatly, sharply and elegantly rendered calligraphy transform each folio into a miniature painting of great beauty.

A folio of *Zafar-Namah*
Sikh, Punjab, dated A.D. 1872
Paper, 30 x 20 cm, Acc. no: M/824
Collection: Punjab Archives, Patiala.
*Zafar-namah, or the epistle of victory, the widely known poetic letter of the Tenth Guru
to the Mughal emperor Aurangzeb written in Persian in 1705 from Dina Kangarh contains 58 folios.
It is an illustrated copy and its illustrations and calligraphy are believed
to have been done by Rajaram Tota.*

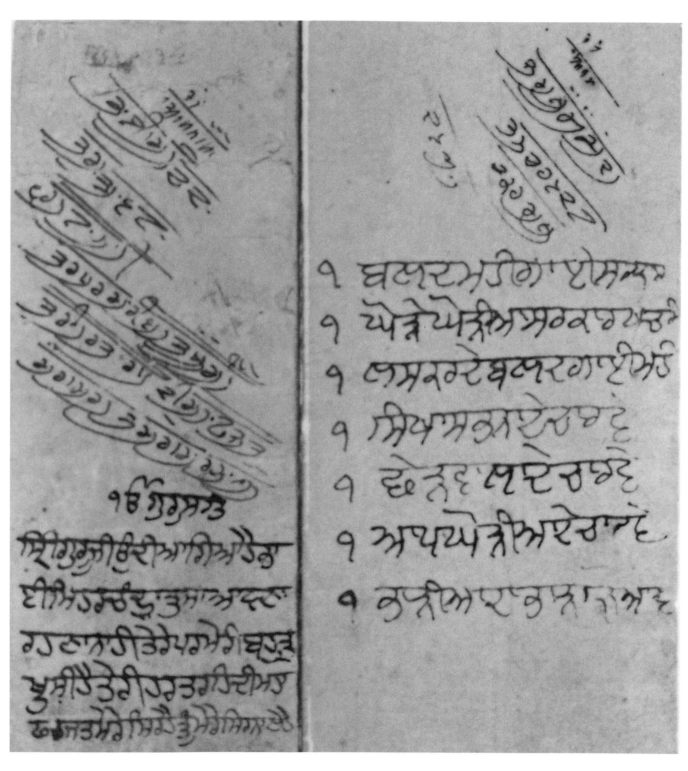

(Above right) RUKKA, A WRITTEN MESSAGE FROM GURU GOBIND SINGH TO BHAI RUPA
Paper, 13.4 x 11.7 cm, Script and language: Gurmukhi

(Above left) HUKAM-NAMAH FROM GURU GOBIND SINGH TO BHAI MIHIR CHAND OF VILLAGE BHAI RUPA
Paper, 13 x 5 cm, end of 17th century
Collection: Bhai Suchet Singh, village Bhai Rupa, Moga, Punjab
This Hukam-namah has been addressed to Bhai Mihir Chand of the village Bhai Rupa.
Guru Gobind Singh has asked him to join him as he and his benefaction has always been
his deep concern - teri har tarah di muhafzat mere sir hai, tu mere sir nal hai.

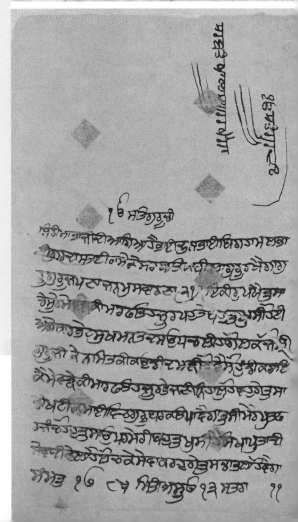

Hukum-Namas, a written *ruqqa* or an official communication for administrating affairs of the state, or estate, a material instrument of worldly ends, had in Sikh traditon a role as signficant as had commandments in Christianity and *Firmans* in Islam. *Hukum-Namas* were issued to a *sangat* or Sikhs directing them to do as required. It could be anything, propagation of *Panth*, raising funds, serving at *langars*, or at *car-sewa*, arranging Gurus' tours, their stay and congregations and ensure attendance on an occasion, or whatever was required for the smooth functioning of the *Panth*. *Hukum-Namas* acquired so far reveal that they were also used for asking *sangats* and Sikhs to celebrate a particular festival or occasion or attend some special *sangat* in *Guru-Darbar* and for such objects as helped maintain *Panth's* unity, conveyed Gurus' appreciation of a Sikh or *sangat,* or their displeasure, or announced cancellation of a programme. *Hukum-Nama* is still the most potent instrument of the Sikh-*Panth*. In the Sikh ecclesiastical system such *Hukum-Namas* are issued now by the five *Takhts*, the *Akal-Takht* at Amritsar, the *Takht* Sri Kesgarh Sahib at Anandpur Sahib, *Takht* Harmandir Sahib at Patna, *Takht Sachkhand* at Nanded and *Takht Damdama*

Sahib at Talwandi Sabo.

The *Hukum-Namas* issued from time to time by Sikh Gurus, and later by eminent Sikhs like Banda Bahadur, Mata Sundari and Mata Sahib Devi are, besides their Panthic significance, a potent source of Sikh history. All *Hukum-Namas* of the Sikh Gurus were issued under their orders and dictated by them but reported ones reveal that most of them were inscribed by regular scribes though authenticated by them. Sometimes Gurus wrote a few words in their own hand and left the rest to scribes to complete.

Guru Hargobind and Guru Tegh Bahadur, however, issued their *Hukum-Namas*, in their own hand. Most of the *Hukum-Namas* of the sixth Guru Hargobind and the nineth Guru Tegh Bahadur are believed to have been written in their own hands. As claims Dr. Ganda Singh, 18 of the 22 of the *Hukum-Namas* of these Gurus are in their own hand. Some of the *Hukum-Namas* of Guru Tegh Bahadur begin with a few words in his hand and the rest in that of the scribe. These *Hukum-Namas*, to the extent of their containing Gurus' hand-writing, are of the status of relics, though more than that they are the most trusted historical record of past providing an insight into the growth-process of Sikh ethics, ecclesiastical management and various Sikh institutions.

Different from the earlier Prophets who founded faiths or sects, but hardly ever a house, or a seat, for perpetuating from it their thought, the Sikh Gurus sought to create material entities-books, buildings, ponds, *baolis*, and weapons, and to attach to them spiritual sanctity transforming each one into a mirror of the Divine. Simple and obvious seems to be the reason. They believed this material fold itself contained means to soul's liberation. Instead of, hence, detesting they sought to discover in a material entity its such inherent capacities which helped uphold the faith and worked first its own sublimation and then soul's spiritual elevation.

Sikh Gurus' architectural activities and laying townships had begun with Guru Nanak's converting the house of Sajjan Thag into a *dharmshala* and founding beside the river Ravi his seat and the town by the name of Kartarpur. Constructional work with a definite objective was, however, begun by Guru Amardas at Goindwal in the form of *baoli*. Imbuing it with spiritual significance Guru Amardas laid the foundation of Sikhs' holy architecture assigned to serve a three-fold purpose-serving people's practical needs, giving Sikhs a geography, and elevating them spiritually. Guru Ramdas, when constructing

THE GOLDEN TEMPLE
Sikh, Punjab, end of 19th century
Collection: Govt. Museum and Art Gallery, Chandigarh.

ponds, the *Amrit-sar* and *Santokh -sar*, and the town Ramdaspur, had in his mind the standards laid by his predecessor. The very site he chose for constructing *Amrit-sar*, the pond with nectar, had associated with it the myth that it was endowed with nectaral properties of curing from several fatal ailments variedly in its water collected over there, in some herb growing around, or in a tree.

Though the vision of a saint meant to provide Sikhs with a spiritual home, Ramdaspur, or Chak Ramdas, was a well considered step towards creation of not only a town but also a seat for Sikh faith. The selection of the site on the country's most highly used highway and acquisition of land by way of purchase for a sum of Rs. 700.00, or even by way of gift from emperor Akbar, could not be just casual. Guru Ramdas is known to put special efforts to bring to Ramdaspur traders, artisans, money-lenders and other professional. Obviously, he wished to generate amongst his Sikhs greater confidence by giving them a land of their own and attract to this Sikhist fold as many people as possible.

It was, however, during the period of the fifth Guru Arjan that Sikhs' more significant architectural activities prevailed. Guru Arjan deepend, widened and fortified the pond, *Amrit-sar*, expanded the town and completed

111

whatever his father Guru Ramdas had left incomplete and built in the centre of the pond Sikhs' holiest and the most significant shrine, Sri Hari Mandir and enlivened it by installing in it the 'light' of the Gurus, their *bani* compiled as the sacred *Adi-granth*. It is said, Guru Arjan in consultation with Baba Buddhaji, himself prepared the design of the holy structure and imbued it with deep spiritual significance. Keeping with the secular spirit of the *Panth* the known *Sufi* saint Mian Mir was brought to lay its foundation. It was thenafter that Ramdaspur came to be known as Amritsar after the name of the sacred pond Guru Ramdas had built.

Most of the construction of Hari Mandir was carried out voluntarily by Guru's followers, Guru Arjan himself supervising constantly. Everything in the temple's design seemed to have a meaning. It had a low plinth suggesting Sikh *Panth's* humility and a humble base. It was by and large made to remain a simpler structure, its devotee's left to seek its magnificence in the intensity of their own devotion and the magnitude of their faith. It opened on all four sides for its protective eye extended its *nazar, kirpa,* its benevolence, its compassion to all alike, provided access to all whatever their caste, creed, or origin, and all directions poured into it their light, though only after such light had undergone its own purgation by passing across its holy waters. It was linked with the world beyond the pond but by a single causeway for there was but one passage to reach **Him**, and the passage was from over the waters, which souls heavy with sins, impurties and conceit, failed to tread.

Hari Mandir, a temporal centre of spiritual elevation and divine realisation defining Sikhs spiritual geography and their holiest seat of pilgrimage, was a constant prey of the attacks of Islamic invaders who had somehow great antipathy against this shrine. In 1764 it was almost pulled down by Ahmed Shah Abdali and had to be reconstructed. A confederation of Sikh misldars and chieftains under Sardar Jassa Singh Ahluwalia reconstructed it between 1764 to 1778. Some 40-50 years after it Maharaja Ranjit Singh got the exterior of the shrine almost completely renovated and covered with gold-plated copper leaves which gave

112

GURDWARA BABA ATAL

Gurdwara Baba Atal is situated south-east ot the Golden Temple at Amritsar.
It is a nine storey octagonal tower built in memory of nine years old Baba Atal Rai,
the deceased son of the sixth Guru Hargobind. He had passed away
at the age of nine out of repentence performing a miracle realising that
it was against the spirit of Sikhism.

it the name *Swaran Mandir,* or Golden Temple. The Golden Temple is now the apex of Sikh architecture and constructed by the divine hands is as holy as *Sri Guru Granth Sahib,* no other object falling in the line.

Guru Hargobind later built in the precinct of Hari Mandir *Akal Takht,* a large building to serve as Sikhs' supreme political seat and a fortress at Amritsar, the first defence structure of Sikhs. Though they have their own importance in the growth of Sikh architecture, yet they are not so much the objects of reverence as is the Golden Temple. Sikh Gurus were more interested in founding cities. Besides earlier Nanak's Kartarpur, Guru Amardas' Goindwal and Guru Ramdas' Chak Ramdas, Guru Arjan founded the towns of Kartarpur in Jullundar Doab, Tarantaran with a large *dharmshala* and a leprosarium and Sri Hargobindpur named after his son. The sixth Guru Har Gobind himself founded the town of Kiratpur and Guru Teg Bahadur Anandpur Sahib. Sikh Gurus did not give up household life, yet no Sikh Guru is known to have built a house for himself considering, perhaps, that sky was his canopy and horizons the four walls of his house.

The Sikh architecture, pursuing more or less the line that Sikh Gurus had taken, is comparatively a simpler thing with little archi-tectural merit or attributes defining it. Even antiqueness does not characterize a Sikh monument for it is a thing of just recent past undergoing recurring renovations or alterations and even *Swaran Mandir* is not any exception to it. As for Gurus' cities, or others, they grow and change their faces every tenth-fifteenth year. The magnificence of Sikh architecture is to be sought hence in its spiritual sanctity, its power, its strength to lead Sikhs to unity along the path of righteousness and to in-spire in them reverence to God and *His* house. To a Sikh a Gurdwara is not a marval of building art. It is above all buildings for it is the house of *Him* who is above us all. Not so much the splendour as piety defines Sikh architecture. A robust Sikh head is seen bowing wherever stands a mast, or a pole with a Sikh flag, the sacred *Nishan Sahib*, crowning it, whether amidst the splendour or barren lands, for it inspires his reverence and speaks of *His* divine presence.

Sacred Relics and other Objects

◆

Sikhism did not approve idol worship, but held in deity-like reverence things known to have remained associated with their Gurus, or formed part of spiritual sanctity, elevating them to status of timeless, formless entity, though such things were subject to decay, decomposition and change. These things, by virtue of their association with the Gurus or *Panth*, moved a Sikh emotionally generating in him a feeling of devotion towards his Gurus and a commitment towards his *Panth*. It is partly in such things that Punjab has its sectarian unity and a recourse to spiritualism for in such material forms, its deep devotional mind apperceives the presence of formless, timeless Supreme and its Gurus, guiding and commanding it to the path of righteousness.

The entire Sikh world, within and beyond the boundaries of Punjab, has as an invaluable legacy of past several things, most religiously and meticulously preserved and protected by generations of Sikhs, from Nanak's *sailly, topi, kamandal* and *gudari* to Guru Govind Singh's *kalam*, sword and pair of shoes which the tradition believes and revers as to have once belonged to their Gurus. The genuineness of a Sikh's faith and his emotional attachment to these objects renders insignificant the question whether they were genuine or otherwise, for a thing fake could not so long and so massively move a community to so pious feelings of devotion and reverence. In Sikhs' genuine faith lies their genuineness.

Besides such personal belongings of the Gurus, other things, though composed materially alike of elements to decompose and change, which stood for something beyond their material meaning, were as much revered and imparted alike spiritual sanctity and a status beyond time. They were revered as sacred and sometimes as divine for they transported a Sikh to a realm different from his own. *Rabbab*, by virtue of its association with the Sikh tradition from the very inception of such tradition, has been to a Sikh a sacred instrument but the *Nishan Sahib*, concieved initially by Guru Hargobind as a pennant to enthuse his Sikhs and soldiers with a champion's spirit, far above a material thing, is a

PADUKAS OF GURU GOBIND SINGH

(Opposite page top) BATA SAHIB, THE BOWL OF GURU GOBIND SINGH
Collection: S. Balbir Singh, Jora Sahib, Nangal
Faridkot, Punjab.

divine entity, an institution of Sikh faith. After the birth of *Khalsa Khanda*, the symbol of might, was added to crown it, which imparted to the *Nishan Sahib* such sanctity that its very presence consecrated any place as a holy shrine but without its holy presence no building, whatever its structure, could attain the status of a shrine.

Military spirit was as much a Sikhist legacy as was its spiritualism, one bringing to it strength and splendour, the other its thought and piety. Hence, weapons symbolising might, military spirit and a Sikh's inner strength were held in great reverence since the days of Guru Arjan. After the birth of *Khalsa* two of them, *Khanda* and *Kirpan*, one the instrument of preparing by its touch the baptizing *amrit*, the nectar, and the other constituting one of the five physical attributes, the emblems of a Sikh's identity, were consecrated into the holy tradition as Sikh's sacred objects. Guru Gobind Singh had used *Khanda* for stirring the *sharbat* with which he baptized to *Khalsa* his first five Sikhs and himself. Since then

Khanda was not a mere weapon but an essential organ of baptizing to *Khalsa*. *Khanda* symbolised an instrument, which transformed by its touch simple water into nectar and a simple folk into the purest one. A simple weapon was thus transformed into a spiritual instrument of sectarian conversion and had become the symbol of guided strength and resolute mind. This *Khanda* was later made to crown the *Nishan Sahib* and with a couple of *Kirpans*, to serve now for three hundred years now as *Panth's* emblem.

Khalsa made a few more material objects respectable to a Sikh. A member of the community of *Khalsa* was required to be absolutely pure and observe a code of conduct and to adhere to a certain mode of personal living with some physical

attributes prescribed apparently for their identity as Sikhs. These attributes had otherwise too a deeper significance and guided a Sikh's life from his head to toe. The turban added to head's physical height, held it high and by its spiral shape led mind to incline upward to ever-greater heights. The comb, *Kanga*, weeded out evil and undesirable. The *Kara* clutched a hand to right doing and abstaining from wrong, and its touch, transformed food into Gurus' bounty. The *Kirpan*, or sword, protected and preserved the right and eradicated wrong. Perched on waist with upward handle it required mind to hold it and with its downward blade it aimed at cleansing and purifying the earth. *Kachchha* inspired grace and modesty.

115

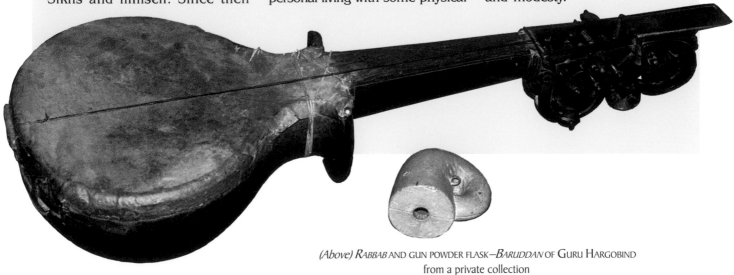

(Above) RABBAB AND GUN POWDER FLASK—BARUDDAN OF GURU HARGOBIND
from a private collection

(Left) THE *KATAR* OF GURU GOBIND SINGH
Steel, 38 x 7.5 cm, Acc. no.: 67, Collection: Qila Mubarak, Patiala.
Guruji to Bhai Tiloka gifted this Katar when he was baptised along with his brother Ram Singh at
Damdama Sahib in 1705. Though the Katar is largely inscribed in Persian, yet out of such inscription only
its date, Samvat 1752 that is 1695 and 'Gobind Singh....Shah- i-Shahan...Teg' is readable.

(Above) SCRUBBER OF GURU HARGOBIND
(Below right) A *KACHHERA* OR UNDER GARMENT OF SIXTH GURU
(Below left) *GAGAR* OF GURU HARGOBIND
Collection: Bhai Rattan Singh of Daroli Bhai, Moga, Punjab.

Faithful Visions of the Divine

Janam-Sakhis and Illustrated copies

Janam-sakhis, meaning a life as witnessed, ordinarily the fictions depicting legends of Baba Nanak's life cropped up during the early centuries of his birth, represent the faithful vision of the Divine. Different from a set of chronological data or a biography, the *Janam*, as the faithful mind bears witness, the *sakshya* to, is such mind's own creation beyond a time-frame and beyond how the born one had actually lived, a vision of the mind emotionally and devotionally attached to.

The term *sakhi* as used here is not much different from the Sanskrit *sakshi* meaning the all pervading mind as also the mind perceiving **Him**, though it has greater affinity with Kabir's *sakhi* where it sometimes means a vision born of an emotionally attached mind and sometimes the knowing intuitive eye that transports a vision from beyond to within, from material to spiritual, to better apprehend it:

Sakhi ankhin gyan ki, samajhi dekhi mana mahin.
Bin sakhi sansar kau jhagara nibatata nahin,

that is., unless the 'Knowing eye' carries the vision from beyond to within and realises **Him**, the enigma, the mystery of the universe, is not resolved, nor transcendence beyond the cycle of birth and death is attained. In Sanskrit *sakshya* or *pramana* is another name given to *Puranas* and sometimes contemplated as its root-term, that is, *Puranas*, or the *sakshya*, bear witness to **Him**. And, centuries of faith acclaim that by absorbing within the *sakshya*, which the *Puranas* contemplate, the self is redeemed from the pangs of life and death. The *Jatakas* in the Buddhist tradition accomplished an alike

117

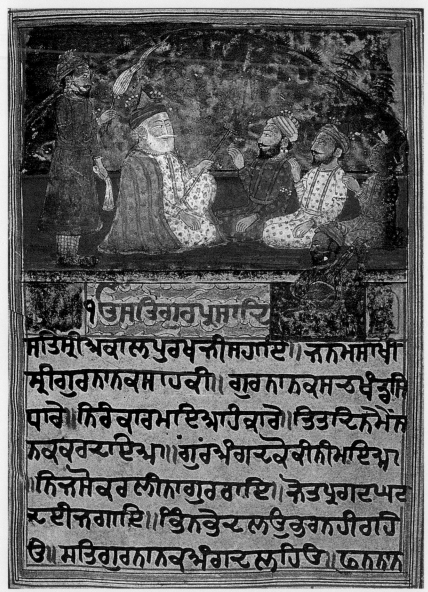

GURU NANAK WITH BHAI BALA AND MARDANA
The first folio of a Janam Sakhi
Sikh, Punjab, end of 18th century
Paper, Acc. no: 75.658
Collection: National Museum, New Delhi.

object. It seems obvious that *Janam-Sakhis* were conceived, quite possibly like *Puranas* and *Jatakas*, as *sakshya* to the divine birth, and as a means to salvation and for unveiling the enigma, the mystery of the universe. *Janam-sakhis* are thus, like *Puranas* and *Jatakas*, the faithful vision of the Divine realized within for *'bin sakhi sansar kau jhagara nibatata nahin'*.

Janam-sakhis are as popular and sacred in the Sikh tradition, as are *Puranas* in Brahmanical and *Jatakas* in Buddhist. In Gurmukhi *sakhi* is supposed to mean 'stories' for to the popular mind *Janam-sakhis* are the life stories of Baba Nanak. The chronology of the *Janam-sakhis* or the date when the first *Janam-sakhi* was created is not known. However, it is evidenced from one of the *varan* written by Bhai Gurdas, a disciple of Guru Arjan and the scribe of the *Adi-granth* that there was a well-developed *Janam-sakhi* tradition in vogue during the tenure of the fifth Sikh Guru. During the later half of the 16th and the entire 17th century a number of *Janam-sakhis* came into being, each with a different set of anecdotes, different chronology, different vision and a different tradition. Works like *Janam-sakhis, Puratan Janam-sakhi, Mehraban's Sachkhand Pothi*, Bhai Mani Singh's *Gian Ratnavali* and *Janam-sakhi* of

Bala appear to attempt at re-counting the life story of Guru Nanak, though each one save an unanimity as regards the details of his birth, parentage, family and its links, travel accounts and his discourse during such travels with *yogis, sadhus* etc. has its own vision of him, obviously, for the being they wrote of was different in each one's case. He was each time re-born in the faithful mind.

Some of the *Janam-sakhis*, or narratives, are quite fanciful even attributing miracles to Guru Nanak, while the others appear to unveil, from behind such fancifulness, a philosophic or religious message. There are many that incorporate in them a hymn, series of couplets or other quotations, the narrative part serving only as their scene setting. Their language is mostly Punjabi, script *Gurmukhi* and the diction fiction in prose, imbuing them with exceptional vigour experienced in a story book. Thus, with a common man's diction and fictional style *Janam-sakhis* have always made an interesting reading, and with their religious significance and the message which they have been imparting, they have always guided and inspired the devotional mind of Sikhs. Alike, *Janam-sakhis* are found both, simple plain manuscribed texts and as also highly illustrated, serving both, the ordinary as well an affluent Sikh. *Janam-sakhis* thus

(Above left) BABA NANAK LISTENING TO MARDANA'S *RABBAB*
Sikh–Pahari mix style, end of 18th century
Paper, 14.5 x 8.3 cm
Collection: S.S. Hitkari, New Delhi.

(Left) RAJA MADHURBAIN COMES TO PAY HOMAGE TO GURU NANAK
Sikh–Pahari mix style, dated A.D. 1793
Paper, 22.6 x 16.5 cm, Acc. no.: 4072
Collection: Govt. Museum and Art Gallery, Chandigarh.
A leaf from the series depicting the life events of Baba Nanak inscribed as:
'Sakhi raie Madhurbain nal hoi'.

have always created a bridge amongst cross-sections of Sikhs. Incidentally, *Janam-sakhis* illustrations mark the beginning of Sikh paintings. Despite such a treasure as *Janam-sakhis* are, meticulously preserved, protected and handed over by one generation of Sikhs to the other, it is painful to note that they are not even properly documented.

The Sikh art, portrait, frescoes, border illumination, decorative designs, has its seeds in *Janam-sakhi* illustrations. In Sikh art *Janam-sakhi* illustrations are the earliest. Though serializing or narrating the significant events of Guru Nanak's life, these illustrations lay greater emphasis on portrayal, high-lighting Guru Nanak's personality aspect as it prevailed, or underwent changes in people's mind from time to time. Sobha Singh, a known artist of the recent past, preferred to portray him with a turban instead of his usual *topi* for by Sobha

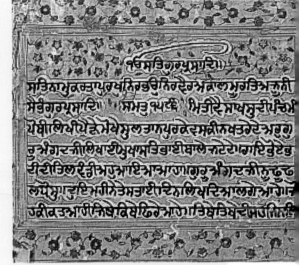

Singh's own time a turban had come to be a Sikh's principal identity mark, hence of his first Guru. In a way Sobha Singh rendered in Guru Nanak's form his own vision of him. Guru Nanak's dynamism, multiprofiles of face, regalia including nimbus and attendants with flywhisks, saintliness, facial sublimity, his costumes, rosary, *tilaka*, shash and locations of his seat befitting his Prophet's form, have been aptly rendered in these illustrations.

In landscapic settings he is depicted seated under a tree, near a river or against a terrain, but when in a dwelling on a carpet or a sheet of cloth laid on a bedecked floor. A *saili*, *topi*, rosary, long *jama* or *kurta*, a shash, *tilaka*, nimbus, a *simarini*, a benign smile, the face turned slightly to right or to left, are the usual features that artists illustrating *Janam-sakhis* rendered. From his *topi* seems to rediate a circle of light, something like a divine aura symbol-

izing his enlightened state. In *Janam-sakhi* illustrations cap is an essentiality, though painted variedly, as conical, close fitting and sometimes his best-known *qalandari*. A shawl or *chadar* on his shoulder painted to enhance dignity of his bearing is sometimes replaced by a *gudari* symbolical of Kabir's all assimilating bearing, humility, all embracing, all pervading expanses of his life and mission.

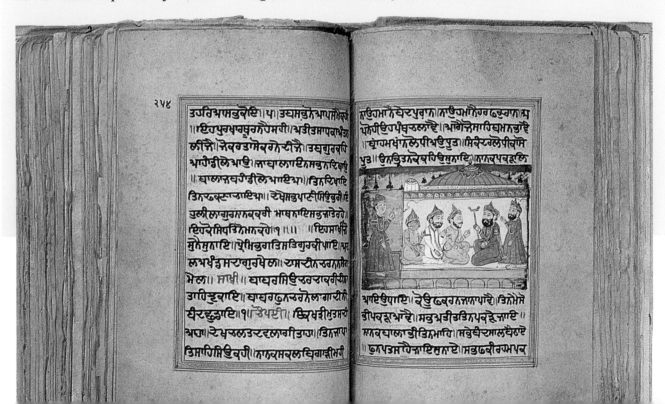

GURU NANAK WITH BHAI BALA AND MARDANA

(Right) OM WITH FIGURES OF BRAMHA-SARAWATI, VISHNU-LAKSHMI AND SHIVA-PARVATI
Sikh–Bikaner mix style, Punjab, a Persian manuscript of circa A.D. 1830
Illustrations: 53, Folios: 136
Paper, 28.5 x 15.5 cm, Acc. no: 1035/3
Collection: Maharaja Ranjit Singh Museum, Amritsar.
*The opening page of the Military Manual of Maharaja Ranjit Singh
with Bikaneri art features dominating it is very likely that this manuscript
was illustrated by some artist from Bikaner.*

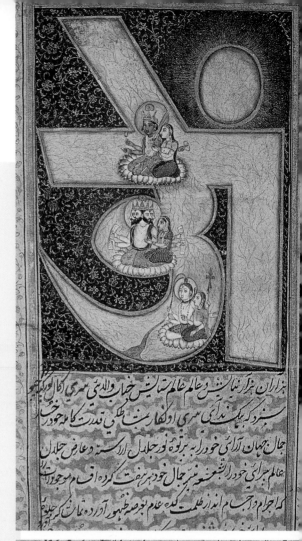

The Military Manual of Maharaja Ranjit Singh, a Persian manuscript with 136 folios, 53 painted and other 83 plain, is apparently a military guideline laid down for training his soldiers and modernizing forces much on the lines of French 'Manuel de Cavelerie', though different from it Maharaja Ranjit Singh's Manual has imbued, in its illustrated part at least, a deep spiritualism rare even to religious texts. This Manual, before anything else, begins by dedicating its first folio to three Brahmanical gods with consorts riding the mystic syllable **OM** and devotes another ten for rendering Ten Sikh Gurus' portraits, as if symbolizing that the Manual essentially leads arms to spiritualism rather than to blood-shed, or that recourse to bloodshed could only occasion when nationhood, sainthood or righteousness were in peril. It is not for its decorative worth that the Brahmanical gods have been rendered against the background of mystic syllable **OM**. With his deeper faith in Guru Nanak's vision of the Supreme the artist seems to convey that all formative visions of the Divine are born of the formless syllable capable of expanding into any form, dimension and discipline, and, thus, conveyed the supremacy of the *bani*, and that of *simaran*, the subtlest means of **His** realisation.

All the Ten Gurus are deified in customary regal bearing, nine rendered seated on golden *chawkis* with *morchhal* bearers attending, the nimbus defining their divinity. The Tenth Guru Gobind Singh, the prime source of inspiration of Maharaja Ranjit Singh's military spirit, has been painted riding a stallion with regalia around. The colours, bright but simple, have been so used that they appropriately project each one's personality in a distinctive way. The next folio depicts Maharaja Ranjit Singh who advanced the great legacy of Sikh Gurus through out his life and in all his deeds. His Military Manual, more than the transcription of his army management, is his tribute to the Divines.

(Right) MAHARAJA RANJIT SINGH WITH HIS FRENCH COURTIERS
VANTURA AND ALLARD AND SOME SIKH NOBLES

(Above left) SOLDIERS
All the folios are from the *Military Manual*

Gulgashat-i-Punjab

ulgashat-i-Punjab, a Persian manuscript with 286 folios of which 23 are illustrated, scribed by Pandit Raja Ram Kaul Tota, reflects an effort at creating a new historic era to begin with 1469 when with the birth of Guru Nanak Punjab underwent a renaissance to 1849, the date of its completion. *Gulgashat-i-Punjab* comprises of all significant events of the lives of the Ten Sikh Gurus, their brief life-sketches and a detailed chronology of the era of Maharaja Ranjit Singh highlighting the factors responsible for the rise and fall of the Sikh empire during his life-time and after his death. Different from a mere factual history the manuscript records Punjab's spiritual journey through this passage of some 400 years.

The illustrated part comprises mainly of the designs and sketches of the monuments of Lahore and Amritsar, the most important of them all being the colour sketch of the Golden Temple with its surrounding buildings, the *Akal-Takht*, the causeway leading to Harmandir Sahib and the holy *sarovara*. The Akal Bunga and the Bungas of Raja Dhiyan Singh, Kanwar Nau Nihal Singh, Maharaja Ranjit Singh, Maharaja Sher Singh, Jamadar Khushal Singh and Ramgarhias, the tower of Baba Atal, Gobindgarh fort, part of Lahore fort, as also the Mughal buildings constructed inside it by Mughal emperors, the tomb of Anarkali, some mosques and gardens, the Kangra fort and the temple of goddess Jwalamukhi situated near Kangra, some private mansions, are other types of

(Top) GOLDEN TEMPLE AND ITS SURROUNDINGS
Sikh, Punjab, dated A.D.1849
Scribe: Raja Ram Kaul Tota, Illustrations: 23, total folios: 286
Script: Nasta'liq, Language: Persian
Paper, 36 x 22.5 cm, Acc. no: 7
Collection: Maharaja Ranjit Singh Museum, Amritsar.
Gulgasht-i-Punjab meaning a passage across the land of flowers
is a historical record of Punjab from 1469 to 1849 comprising of the main
political events and the phases of the growth of Sikh Panth.

122

(Below) Maharaja Kharak Singh and his son Kunwar Nau Nihal Singh

(Bottom) The Tomb of Anarkali
The illustration is inscribed on its top as
Naksha-i-makabara-e-Anarkali al-asare kanizak Hazrat Akbar Badshah
that means the tomb of Anarkali,
the specially honoured maid of Mughal emperor Akbar.
(Both folios are from Gulgashat-i-Punjab)

structures sketched in the manuscript. *Gulgashat-i-Punjab* thus not only records the growth of Sikh architecture and various elements incorporated from other architectural styles but also emphasized its continuity. The manuscript visually documents Punjab's otherwise lesser known architectural heritage.

Gulgashat-i-Punjab displays a multiplicity of approach to its material. Besides historical part, it includes folk element by introducing the *maqbara* of Anarkali, the legendary love of Akbar's son Salim, who later ruled as emperor Jahangir, entombed alive on her refusing to disown her love for emperor's son. *Gulgashat-i-Punjab* has a strong visual aspect representing several significant buildings and important personalities. It includes a decorative tree for a graphic representation of the geneology of Maharaja Ranjit Singh and the Sandhandwalia Misl. In many ways it projects the grandeur and the rich life-style of Maharaja Ranjit Singh's court and his era. Designs, sketches and depictions of monuments and buildings have been rendered in lighter tones of colours whereas portraits are done in brighter ones and with greater embellishment. In many ways in *Gulgashat-i-Punjab* reflects Punjab's own personality distinct and unique cast in the mould of four hundred years of Sikh tradition.

123

Reflections of the Divinity

Reflections of the Divinity

In aestheticism, spontaneous and simple born of experiences, Sikhism sought its prime base and reflection of the Divine. The cosmic phenomenon was Sikh Gurus' Book of the Beautiful and the Sublime, and song, poetry and music conjoint, the subtlest means of aesthetic realisation. They believed that the self within conversed with the Supreme self without through all that is beautiful, true, bountiful and sublime. Hence, in whatever delighted the self they saw the glimpses of the Benevolent Creator. It was long after that they consecrated places and personified entities for worship, which they initially and otherwise sought in **His** created cosmos itself.

Strangely Prophet Mohammad and Guru Nanak in an identical way witnessed in forms the Formless One. When meditating in a cave near desert hill Hira Prophet Mohammad heard a celestial voice commanding him "Read". The dismayed Prophet, for he knew not how to read, looked around, and above, to find but wide writ on the cosmic face **His** message. And, what a miracle, he who did not know how to read was able to

read it. Guru Nanak, when asked at Jagannathpuri to perform *arti*, was dismayed to find when he raised his head to the sky, that the entire universe stood in **His** worship. Nanak saw **His** *arti* went on incessantly, the sky stood converted into a disc containing on it Sun and Moon turned into lamps, multitudes of stars into pearls, winds into incense, vegetation below into flowers and horizons echoed with **His** name. He felt that the entire cosmos throbbed with his divine presence and all that existed seemed to stand in **His** worship. He bowed his head in reverence. He thought how he could lift his own *thal* of *arti* in isolation when as a small fragment of the whole he already was in **His** incessant service, and after he had realised his littleness how he could distinguish himself from **His** entire Creation. As Prophet Mohammad had deciphered **His** word wide writ on the cosmic countenance, so saw Guru Nanak **His** face in the face of the universe and sang enthused to let the divine spirit within him reach the Supreme and converse in perpetuity.

Guru Nanak, and the Sikh tradition in its very inception, took

recourse to 'song' for aesthetic realisation and to feel thereby the presence of the Bountiful, Compassionate, All-doing, All pervading Creator. Contemplating that the entire cosmos represented but only **His** vision and was thus but **His** mere canvas the Sikh Gurus did not initially approve visual representations in art as a means of aesthetic realisation. However, later Gurus, considering a common Sikh's difficulty in seeking his Guru's presence in abstraction, something materially absent, allowed them to have their likenesses recreated though restricting mainly to painting to include frescoes, illustrations, portraits and narratives. Later Maharaja Ranjit Singh introduced textiles, embroidered and woven, metals used as weapons, coins, medals, crowns, ornaments, jewellery, artefacts and items of day-today use and other unconventional things like ivory for rendering Sikh themes and visualising the lives of Gurus and champions of Sikhism as art media, though not admitted in Sikh tradition ever before. Sculptures and idol casting, in consideration of prohibition of idolatry, was, however, yet disallowed in Sikhism.

125

(Opposite page) BABA NANAK IN MEDITATION
Sikh, Punjab, Modern, Oil on canvas
Artist: Jaswant Singh, 1975
Collection: Govt. Museum and Art Gallery, Chandigarh.
This painting marks a departure not only from medieval forms to the modern,
but also from the traditional form of Guru Nanak's portraits.

Sikh Paintings

◆

The Sikh themes- the life-events of Guru Nanak, portraits of Sikh Gurus, ideals of Sikh life and canons of Sikh faith and, of course, textual illuminations characterised the early Sikh painting. The theme rather than style marked a painting as Sikh. Besides that a Sikh painting was thematic it was as essentially spiritual. In Sikhism the 'song' was from its very inception its very core and the subtlest means of aesthetic realisation, but there developed soon in the Sikh tradition its own visual arts, the painting in particular, another significant means of apprehending the aestheticism contained in cosmic harmony and visual phenomenon. The Sikh painting did not render mere copies of objects, whatsoever, but endeavoured rather to discover an object's inner structure, its spirit, its inherent capability to lead the soul to perception of higher beauty and deeper spiritual significance and work thereby aesthetic as well as spiritual elevation, a role which is essentially transcendental.

The illustrations of a *Janam-sakhi* of 1658 reported from P. N. Kapoor of Delhi is the earliest example of Sikh painting. This *Janam-sakhi* is a transcription of an earlier version of Bhai Bala's *Janam-sakhi* by some Gorakhdas. It contains 267 folios of which 29 are painted. These painted folios

serialise some important events of Guru Nanak's life rendered in quite a simple and graphic style, yet capable of initiating a new art form. Another example of Sikh art is seen in the dated copy of the *Adi-granth* of 1666 with only its prefacing folio illuminated. The illumination follows the tradition of Qu'ranic illumination, which was then in great prevalence. This copy, now with the Patiala Archives, Punjab, is otherwise too very significant and also sacred to Sikhs for its prefacing folio contains the *Mul-mantra* in Guru Teg Bahadur's own hand. This copy of the *Adi-granth* suggests that the tradition of illuminating copies of the holy *Adi-granth* had begun as early as mid-17th century. Alike,

there are some portraits depicting Sikh Gurus reported from various sources. Though they are undated, yet stylistically suggestive of mid-17th century. Obviously, the cult of portrait painting in Sikh tradition too had set in almost in simultaneity with narrative serialisation and illumination.

It is thus evident that the Sikh painting, which manifested at its early stage as thematic serialisation, illumination, illustration and portraiture, was in a good state of growth as early as the mid-17th century. And, it is hence erroneous to contend, as most scholars on Sikh art do or rely, that the Sikh painting had its beginning during the regime of Maharaja Ranjit Singh, though it is true

127

(Top) THE *JANAM SAKHI* — TEXT AND ILLUSTRATION
Sikh, Punjab, end of 18th century, Paper, Acc. no: 75.658
Script: Gurmukhi, Folios: 309 Illustrations: 64
Collection: National Museum, New Delhi.

(Opposite page) A PORTRAIT OF GURU GOBIND SINGH
Mandi, Pahari, end of 17th century, Paper, 20 x 18 cm, Acc. no: 71.93
Collection: National Museum, New Delhi.

This portrait seems to have been rendered in 1690s when Guru Gobind Singh visited Mandi and was in all probabilities a personal guest of Raja Siddhasen. As such it amounts to its rare historicity. Its Takri inscription – Guru Gobind Singh, too, is a special feature.

that it was never so much in vogue as during his days. Moreover, it was Maharaja Ranjit Singh who initiated, encouraged and patronised the use of media, other than paper or canvas, which had been widely followed in other non-Sikh art-styles for communicating a Sikh theme. And, it is for such significant role that scholars are led to conclude that the art of painting was Maharaja Ranjit Singh's contribution to Sikh tradition.

Janam-sakhis, though basically the hagiographic texts, weren't merely a significant and cohesive source for Punjab's history after Guru Nanak, or the examples of earliest Punjabi prose, but in their illustration they also poineered what is known today as the Sikh art. The indigenous art of Punjab and its culture that sought its expression in such art were under constant Mughal pressure. But despite *Janam-sakhis*, produced initially mostly by the followers of *Udasi Ramraiya* sect and *Sodhi Deras*, the off-shoots of the mainstream of Sikhism, championed the Sikh cause by their multi-role. *Janam-sakhis* helped the hagiographic growth process of Sikhism, preserved history from Sikh point of view, gave to Punjabi literature its ever first prose and fiction and innovated a new art style characteristically Sikh. The *Janam-sakhis*, thus, stood against the erosive Mughal pressure as Punjab's real buffer strength.

The *Janam-sakhis* continued to have an alike vital role in the growth of Sikh painting during 18th century as well. The Patiala family of Bagarhian is reported to possess a dated *Janam-sakhi* of 1724, which has forty-two illustrated folios almost exactly rendered as the 1658 *Bala Janam-sakhi* of P. N. Kapoor's collection. This 1724 *Janam-sakhi* is also a transcription of an alike earlier copy as is the *Bala Janam-sakhi* of 1658. This 18th century *Janam-sakhi* has been rendered much in the same style and on same kind of paper as has been used for its 17th century counterpart. The possibility, thus, of a common source of both may not be ruled out. These *Janam-sakhis* mark a continuity of Sikh art from mid-17th to the early 18th century. The *Janam-sakhi* with India Office Library, London, widely known as B-40 *Janam-sakhi* of 1734, besides its role in continuing and sustaining the tradition of Sikh painting, has an extra significance. It records exceptionally the names of its illustrating artist and patron. The *Janam-sakhi* with Patiala royal family dateable for 1760 assigns to *Janam-Sakhis* yet another role in enhancing the status of the art of painting in Sikh way. It comprises of 152 paintings of paramount importance and great art merit. These art pieces have been rendered on detached pieces of paper independent of the whole manuscript and appended to it after the text was completed. Obviously, the illustrative part was executed by independent artists or agencies deployed for the purpose. It suggests that the illustrative or the art part of a *Janam-sakhi*, far from being subordinate to text, was as much important and indispensable in *Janam-sakhi* cult as text.

Late 18th and 19th centuries seem to have produced a huge bulk of *Janam-sakhis*. It is noticeable that the number of illustrations was larger each time. The *Janam-sakhi* with the National Museum, New Delhi, titled as *Guru Nanak ki Janam-sakhi*, dated for 1777, is a significant one of this phase. It is a mix of Pahari and Kashmir styles with 670 folios, 3 illuminated and 72 illustrated. The Patiala royal family has in its personal collection another *Janam-sakhi* of 1780 with 137 folios, which contain 82 paintings, a good number for a text of such size. The *Janam-sakhi* of 1793, reported in Roop Lekha (vol. xxxix) from some private collection and some painted leaves of another *Janam-sakhi* and an independent set of similar drawings, both with the Govt. Museum and Art Gallery, Chandigarh, are excellent works. The drawings characterised by fine line-work and painted illustrations with balanced colour scheme have great merit. The

Roop Lekha *Janam Sakhi* has been rendered by some Jawahar Singh, a Guler, Pahari artist commissioned by Sikhs' known hero Baba Baghel Singh reputed to storm Delhi and hoist Sikh flag at Red Fort.

The drawings of Chandigarh Museum's *Janam-sakhi*, a large set, assignable to the known Guler artist Ranja and his pupil son Gurusahai rendered under the probable patronage and inspiration of Sardar Jassa Singh Ramgarhia, the known Sikh chief, is a landmark in defining the growth of Sikh painting. The changes seen occurring in the facial features, costumes, head-dresses and attributes like Mardana's *rabbab* constitute an interesting study. It is noticeable that in one of these drawings the features and headgear of Raja Ugarsen have a striking similarity with features and head-dress of Raja Nala in Guler's set of drawings of Nala-Damayanti series. In other drawings the head-dress of Guru Nanak changes as much strikingly. In one drawing he is seen wearing a cap ribboned by a strip of cloth and peacock feathers, in the other he is in a *topa*, or a crown-cap, though in all of them the feeling of blissful calm and divine glow but without halo alike define his face. In slender waist, sharp features, transparent drapery and ornamentation female figures of these drawings

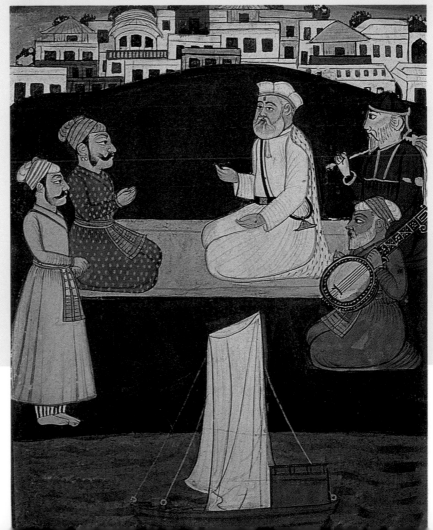

have great similarity with the figures of Ranja's Guler *Ramayana*-set, now with Bharat Kala Bhawan, Varanasi. A *Janam-sakhi* of 1797 comprising of 583 folios with 106 illustrations rendered in an admixture of Pahari and Kashmir styles and scribed in a mixture of *Braj* and *Gurmukhi* reported from Kabul suggests that the tradition of illustrative *Janam-sakhis* was wide spread encompassing the north-west frontiers beyond the river Sutlej.

The *Janam-sakhis* thus, gave Sikh art its theme-all its imaginative stretch and expanse, its entire fictional dimensions, all spiritual concern and all devotional tint. They gave Sikh art its style-portraiture, crystallizing events, arresting movement, narration and serialization, landscape, all motifs and symbols, colours' balance, minuteness, refinement defining borders, margins and other graphic renderings, imbuing in visual forms the invisible spirit and in personal likenesses the appropriate personality aspects and all that was required for

discovering and re-discovering in a theme its inherent message and object. They gave to Sikh art its unity, continuity, coherence, character and art-tradition; and, above all, a capacity to prevail against extraneous pressures and influences and find its own form and base.

The tradition of embellishing *Sri Guru Granth Sahib*, save a few manuscripts reported from the 19th century, remained restricted mostly to its illumination in floral designs, scrolls, arabesques, graphic and geometric patterns and motifs widely in Qu'ranic fashion. Idolatry yet stood prohibited in Sikhism. Hence, after the Holy Book had been deified, figural representations could not have much place in this supreme document of the *Panth*, or at least such liberty as was required for artistic innovations or for the imagination to stretch could not be availed. Hence, the illustrative side of *Sri Guru Granth Sahib* or the *Adi-granth* did not develop. It was quite late around the middle of 19th century that a few illustrated copies of the Holy Book

seem to have been prepared. It becomes evident from such richly illustrated copy of *Sri Guru Granth Sahib* reported from the National Museum, New Delhi. This large size copy lavishly rendered in bright colours and using liberally a good amount of gold prepared for some Sodhi Bhan Singh has some excellent illustrations of great artistic merit.

Frescoes and murals formed a well-established art tradition in India since ancient days. After Islamic invaders began demolishing religious shrines in Indian subcontinent the tradition of frescoes or murals based construction of religious buildings weakened. The construction of shrines itself shifted to far-off secluded and naturally protected sites where chances of invasions were minimum. The early Mughals were somewhat liberal towards Indian arts and religions but in total the Mughal era encouraged or even engineered demolition of Indian shrines, though in their own buildings they preferred frescoes and murals for decorating their inte-

130

WALL PAINTINGS FROM BABA ATAL AT AMRITSAR
Different scenes depicting life events of Guru Nanak
*These frescoes of Baba Atal suggest that the tradition of embellishing the walls
of the Sikh shrines in Sikh art was widespread and quite massive.*

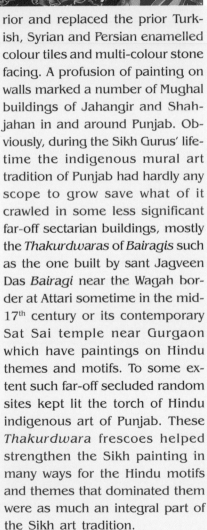

rior and replaced the prior Turkish, Syrian and Persian enamelled colour tiles and multi-colour stone facing. A profusion of painting on walls marked a number of Mughal buildings of Jahangir and Shahjahan in and around Punjab. Obviously, during the Sikh Gurus' lifetime the indigenous mural art tradition of Punjab had hardly any scope to grow save what of it crawled in some less significant far-off sectarian buildings, mostly the *Thakurdwaras* of *Bairagis* such as the one built by sant Jagveen Das *Bairagi* near the Wagah border at Attari sometime in the mid-17th century or its contemporary Sat Sai temple near Gurgaon which have paintings on Hindu themes and motifs. To some extent such far-off secluded random sites kept lit the torch of Hindu indigenous art of Punjab. These *Thakurdwara* frescoes helped strengthen the Sikh painting in many ways for the Hindu motifs and themes that dominated them were as much an integral part of the Sikh art tradition.

This indigenous art of wall painting in Punjab, inclining now decisively to Sikh themes, continued to prevail in simultaneity to other forms of Sikh art along the subsequent stages of its growth. The *samadhi* of Bhai Dalla, a disciple of Guru Gobind Singh who visited Bhai Dalla's house at Talwandi Sabo, now Damdama Sahib, in 1706, some two years before his death, is an important landmark in the development of Sikh art of painting and murals in Punjab. Though largely covered now under the whitewash coating and eroded otherwise too, yet there survive on the interior walls of the *samadhi* some frescoes with Sikh themes dominating. Stylistically and from other collateral evidence these frescoes seem to belong to early part of the 18th century, namely, in between 1706 to 1740. Bhai Dalla's *samadhi* had been constructed in the precincts of Takht Damdama Sahib. The murals in the *samadhi* are the earliest known on Sikh themes and the earliest to use for its inscriptions the *Gurmukhi* script. Though the legends like

those of Shravan Kumar carrying on his shoulders his blind parents to pilgrimage and lord Rama's illustrious sons Lav and Kush defying their own father by holding his sacrificial horse, and secular themes like the one of a teacher and his pupils also figure in these frescoes, yet with prominently rendered portraits of Sikh Gurus alongwith the equestrian portrait of Guru Gobind Singh and other related themes the main thrust of these frescoes is obviously the Sikhism. The significance of these otherwise crude frescoes lies in the variety of theme that they render, in the figurative thrust, thick brush strokes, powerful facial expression and the variedly rendered floral and other motifs. K.C. Aryan has reported in his book 'Punjab Murals' a few other wall paintings of this period from Gurdwara Teg Bahadur at Bahadurgarh (Patiala) opposite the fort. Now only two of them, one portraying Mata Gujari and other Guru Teg Bahadur survive.

Though with some missing links the mural tradition of Punjab

131

seems to have continued during the subsequent phase as well. The Raghunath Temple built in 1750 has now surviving only the faint traces of the contemporary frescoes on its walls. The Hari Mandir seems to have been profusely ornamented with paintings, and of course enamelled too, though consisting only of floral patterns and motifs and no thematic panels, during its reconstruction, which took place in between 1764-1778 after Ahmad Shah Abdali's 1764 attack on the temple. This became evident recently from traces of such old paintings revealed from under the gilded copper plates removed for its renovation. These old murals which the Misldars, while seeking to reconstruct Hari Mandir, got painted pursuing the concurrent fashion of wall paint-

ing, bear witness to the practice of embellishing the walls of shrines though with figurative representations barred in consideration of Sikh view relating to iconolatry. Later Maharaja Ranjit Singh, when seeking to clothe Golden Temple's exterior with gold plated copper sheets and the interior with marble and other semi-precious stones, covered the entire painted surface in its then state under these gilded sheets.

Other 18th century murals reported from other parts of Punjab depict significant stages of the growth of Sikh art of paintings during the 18th century. They include the partially washed paintings on the outside walls of the main shrine of Shri Namdev temple at village Ghoman, sixteen well preserved panels rendered

with Hindu and Sikh themes like the one depicting Guru Nanak with some holy men painted on the walls of *Akhara* Sangalwal built by Mahant Pritam Das at Amritsar near Hari Mandir in Katra Ahluwalia, the panels on the walls of Shivala Buta Ram at Hoshiarpur, better preserved on portico walls and damaged inside the shrine, the paintings on the walls of *Marhi* of Baba Sidh at village Marhi in Faridkot, the paintings on the *samadhi* of Bhai Guddar Singh and Mai Rajji in Dipalpur, Bhatinda and the ten well preserved panels inside the Dera Udasian. These paintings are primitive and hieratic in their style. An admixture of Hindu and Sikh themes characterizes them all. Some of these paintings depict Hindu subjects as well but always with a greater thrust on Sikh themes, Gurus' lives, some of Punjab's love legends and others. These wall paintings strengthen the contention that the practice of embellishing walls of religious establishments, monasteries, *dharmshalas* and temples, with paintings depicting the life-events of Sikh Gurus and their portraits and those of *mahantas* or priests was in great prevalence during the later half of 18th century.

It becomes evident from the remains of these 18th-19th century murals that they followed by and large only various decorative schemes, were mostly formal and

A PORTRAIT OF GURU HARGOBIND
Sikh–Mughal mix style, end of 17th century
Paper, 16.5 x 21 cm
Collection: Bhai Suchet Singh, village Bhai Rupa, Moga, Punjab.
Guru Hargobind was the first Sikh Guru to allow his portrayal.
This portrait, a similar to the one contained in the Kartarpur Adi-Granth,
a manuscript of Guru's own time, now in the possession of the Bedis,
could be close to Guru's likeness and hence has its own significance.

AN EQUESTRIAN PORTRAIT OF GURU HARGOBIND
Sikh–Mughal mix style, end of 17th century
Paper, 35 x 27 cm
Collection: Shri Harish Chander, Chamba, H.P.
*This portrait of Guru Hargobind depicts his likeness similar to his likeness in several
other portraits particularly his equestrian portrait of Dehradun collection of Ram Rai.
It evidences that his likeness had been preserved in Sikh art and affirms that he had been
portrayed during his lifetime. The likeness that his portraits reveal has sharp nose,
heavy muscular body and broad shoulders as his regular features.*

ENRAPT MARDANA LISTENING TO BABA NANAK DELIVERING HIS SPIRITUAL SONG
Mughal, circa A.D. 1740, Paper, 23 x 17 cm
Collection: Bhai Suchet Singh, village Bhai Rupa, Moga, Punjab.
*Mardana was older then Baba Nanak by ten years but as standard practice artist has painted him younger.
The artist of this painting has gone a little ahead and has painted him much younger than the usual practice.
The delicacy and finesse of delineation places the best of Mughal paintings.*

134

MUGHAL EMPEROR BABUR PAYING HOMAGE TO GURU NANAK
Provincial Mughal, Oudh, mid 18th century, Paper, 20 x 27.5 cm
Collection: S.S. Hitkari, New Delhi.
*Though a sheer imaginative rendering, the painting represents the folk tradition that acclaims that the Mughal emperor Babur
had once gone to the darbar of Baba Nanak to pay him his homage. The figure in front of the Baba, whether Babur or whosoever,
is a royal personage attended by a minister and a chauri bearer. Mardana, Baba's constant companion, sits outside,
something which also suggests that the visitor to Baba was someone most distinguished.*

general in nature and were rendered in traditional way with little exceptional or innovative about them. They definitely represent India's dying mural tradition of past, but they lack in vigour, thrust and artistic merit, which marked that great Indian tradition of Ajanta type murals.

The Sikh tradition did not initially have much of visuals and art motifs. Hence, it had to have recourse to Qu'ranic embellishment for its textual illumination, to Mughal art for its finish, refinement and figural perfection and to Hindu art for its themes and art motifs. The Mughal influence on Sikh art came significantly through Ram Rai, the disowned son of Guru Har Rai, who before he migrated to Dehradun and set up there his own Udasi Ram Raiya sect had been for some years at the Mughal court during Aurangzeb's reign. It is noticeable that the portraits of the earlier Sikh Gurus especially those of Guru Hargobind, rendered at Dehradun at the instance of Ram Rai showed a distinct Mughal influence. The equestrian portrait of Guru Har-Gobind from this collection is somewhat queer for the figure of Guruji is larger and heavier than the pony he is riding. Despite Mughal influence these Dehradun portraits lack in compositional balance, finish and finesse such as is seen in other contemporary portraits of Sikh Gurus to include the portrait of Guru Hargobind which an artist of village Sur Singh near Kiratpur is said to have drawn for Guru's relatives and devotees by the consent of the Guru himself. His other significant portraits of this period which define the Sikh art of portraiture include the portrait appended to a copy of the *Adi-granth* now with the Bedis of Kartarpur, an almost exactly similar to it now in the collection of Bhai Suchet Singh of village Bhai Rupa and a few others reported from various private collections. Bhai Suchet Singh, the twelfth in the line of Bhai Rupa, an ardent devotee of Guru Har Gobind, is reported to have in his possession a few fine portraits other than those of Guru Hargobind.

The paintings of Dehradun collection are widely considered to

GURU NANAK SINGS AND MARDANA ACCOMPANIES ON *RABBAB*
Sikh–Pahari mix style, Kangra, circa A.D. 1800
Paper, 19 x 14 cm, Acc. no: 76.35
Collection: National Museum, New Delhi.
*The red conical cap, chaddar with applique design and morchal are the features
peculiar to this painting. Despite damage it retains its colour brilliance.*

belong to the late 17th century. It includes some unique portraits of Guru Nanak in some vital aspects such as are not seen even in subsequent Kangra paintings. Some of them portray him in a semi-profile type tilted face clad in a Mughalia turban and long *jama* with a band around the waist while others in medium size cut-style beard, without nimbus and *simarini*, sometimes seated under a tree on a white sheet. In most of them Mardana with his *rabbab* is seen seated opposite him. His portraits around the end of 17th century are seen undergoing a drastic change. They are rendered now with an exact Mughalia turban with even *Kalgi*, the plume, tugged to it. They do not have the fine execution, well defined and decorated margins and fascinating stylization of the earlier portraits. These earlier portraits of Guru Nanak, both those from Dehradun and the subsequent ones, outstand in their art merit Guru Nanak's portraits rendered later.

The prevalence of paintings on Sikh themes and portraits of Sikh Gurus in Mandi during early 18th century suggests that the geography of the Sikh art had expanded by now beyond the plains of Punjab upto Himalayan region. The Mandi paintings on Sikh themes constitute an interesting study for the minds of those whose hands created them did not do so out of devotion. These paintings are more or less mere professional things little imbued with any kind of spiritualism. W.G. Archer has published in his book 'Indian Paintings from Punjab hills' an early 18th century Mandi style painting dateable between 1700 to 1720 under the caption 'Guru Gobind Singh encounters Guru Nanak'. The painting has four figures, one identified as Guru Gobind Singh and another one as Guru Nanak. Guru Nanak, as identified by Archer, is seen holding a *moorchhal*, something most unusual for Guru Nanak is not known to have ever carried with him a *moorchhal*. Alike the figure Archer identified as Mardana carries in his hands a *sarangi*, again something unusual for Mardana always carried a *rabbab* instead. Obviously, Archer's identification is erroneous. *Moorchhal* and *sarangi* are known to have been the accompaniment of Muslim *darvesh* instead, and many such ones are known to have met Guru Gobind Singh from time to time. A similar painting, though with five figures instead of its four, is reported from the National Museum, New Delhi. Archer is led to such erroneous identification for the artists rendering these paintings failed to cast their figures with that spiritual glow which distinguished a Sikh Guru's figure from other figures.

Guru Gobind Singh is said to have visited the Mandi state in 1697 on an invitation from Mandi's ruler Raja Siddha Sen who after his initial antipathy against Guru Gobind Singh was convinced that he was basically a saint beyond self interests against any Hindu ruler whosoever. Guru Gobind Singh was welcomed with great reverence and hospitality. It explains to a great extent the prevalence of Sikh painting and the construction of a Gurdwara in Mandi State. Raja Siddha Sen, a man of spiritual leanings, was a great connoisseur of art and patronised in his court a team of great artists. May be the artists of his court painted Guru Gobind Singh of their own contemplating their patron's regard for this very special guest, or at the instance of Raja Siddha Sen himself. An unpublished rare portrait of Guru Gobind Singh in the collection of the National Museum, New Delhi, though largely flaked and damaged, aptly explains Raja Siddha Sen's reverence, not merely an amicability, for the Sikh Guru. This Mandi style portrait obviously rendered by a contemporary artist from Mandi, in all probability from Raja Siddha Sen's court and deeply attached to him, represents Guru Gobind Singh exactly as Mandi artists painted their patron Siddha Sen in many of his portraits. The Sikh Guru has been painted with a bow in his hand in the style of Raja Siddha Sen and

(Previous page 135) A PORTRAIT OF GURU NANAK
Deccan, Hyderabad, early 18th century, Paper, 33.5 x 24.5 cm, Acc. no: 59.314
Collection: National Museum, New Delhi.
This boldly treated portraiture of Baba Nanak is essentially in deity form for ritual use
in typical Deccani style. The presence of Mardana with rabbab in a small size figure is
only symbolical. The highly conical cap and choga are typically Deccani.

other hill chiefs. Unless Raja Siddha Sen had held Guru Gobind Singh in high reverence his court artists, or any one from Mandi, would not dare mix the identities of the two into this portrait. This Mandi portrait, being Guru Gobind Singh's contemporary, is significant otherwise too for it could be closer to the Sikh Guru's identity.

By the end of the first half of the 18th century, during Mughal emperor Muhammad Shah's period, Sikh painting seems to have inclined towards the refinement of declining glory of Mughal art. It is widely evidenced from Guru Nanak's portraits reported from Bhai Suchet Singh's collection representing the Sikh Guru in his various aspects, in colourful *qalandari topi*, *Kalagi* etc., and from portraits of other Sikh Gurus of the corresponding period reported from State Museum,

Simla. Besides their early date these portraits powerfully mirror in them the late Mughal and uprising provincial Mughal styles. The known Sikh historian Dr. Ganda Singh claims to have seen amongst the murals of Bal Leela Gurdwara at Nankana Sahib now in Pakistan some similar portraits of Sikh misl chiefs rendered in an alike style and around the same period. It suggests that Sikh art of portraiture did not yet hesitate in pursuing Mughal art models but its theme now, more than ever before, was strictly pure Sikhism. The 18th century Sikh art thus remained dominated by portraiture as its form, Mughal as its style and Sikh as its central theme. It was only by the 19th century that in its use of light and shade and dimensional effects the Sikh art acquired some of the attributes of the European art. The Sikh artists had acquired by now good proficiency in portraying various personality aspects and before the 19th century ended, besides Sikh Gurus, the common Sikh, a labourer, a goldsmith, a weaver, too, had come to be the theme of Sikh portraiture. Flat white background continued till quite late to be the standard backdrop in a Sikh portrait, something which the European impact was able to break to some extent in later ones. Alike a figure's face in profile was the standard but the shoulders and other body part were later ren-

dered tilting to some three-quarters to front.

In the mean time Sikh themes had migrated to other parts of the country, especially to Deccan and Rajasthan where some good paintings portraying the Sikh Gurus were rendered. A portrait of Guru Nanak with Bhai Mardana in typical Deccani (Hyderabad) style has been reported from the National Museum, New Delhi. The composition with Guru Nanak attired as faqir in typical Deccani style gets here an entirely different treatment. For visualising the spiritual height of Guru Nanak different from that of Bhai Mardana the artist has queerly drawn Guru Nanak with a larger figure and Bhai Mardana with quite a short one. The Rajasthani painters too painted Guru Gobind Singh in his various aspects but more so his journeys. A Rajasthani painting of the late 18th century reported from S.S. Hitkari depicts him on his journey to the south. But despite that the Sikh art experimented with various styles, it was never bereft of Mughalia art attributes. A painting of around this period depicting Baba Nanak, which the National Museum, New Delhi had purchased from Wazir Kartar Singh of Nurpur in 1976, though its upper right corner considerably damaged in fire, powerfully evidences the continuity of Mughal impact on Sikh art till quite late in the 19th century. Guru

GURU RAMDAS, THE FOURTH MASTER
Sikh, Punjab, circa A.D. 1740
Paper, 24.9 x 16.5 cm, Acc. no: 74.285
Collection: State Museum, Simla, H.P.

Nanak is in a peculiar *qalandari topi* with a white scarf bordering and Bhai Mardana in typical Mughalia turban and a long *jama*. The *chaddar* having colourful patchwork, used for covering the shoulders of Guru Nanak, is a new addition to Sikh art. Bhai Mardana's *rabbab* is typically similar to the instrument widely used in Kangra Ragamala painting series of late 18th century.

The 19th century, before it ended, had thus greatly diversified Sikh art—its vision, theme, style, area, effects, motifs and symbols, and its entire character. It had no doubt retained its earlier professional angle and sectarian direction but had developed besides secular and amateur aspects. The portrayal of the common man and the depiction of his day-to-day life marked an enormous bulk of art activity of the last two decades of 19th century and the first few of the 20th. Such art sought neither much satisfaction or inspiration in religion nor any gratification in a patron's taste, liking, or connoisseurship. It was a phase when the artist discovered himself, his own essential being, his commonness in his art and felt delighted over his discovery of himself. After he had known himself everything unveiled to his vision its truth, and his quest for re-creating it bred in him a reverence, a commitment to the truth as he had realised it in his vision.

The art now was not confined to illustrating writs, texts, or legends, or translating into lines and colours mere conventions, creeds, or traditions. It sought to reveal its own aestheticism, its own delight and its own truth of a thing, or being. Beliefs were re-looked, conventions and creeds re-appropriated and past re-searched and re-constructed. This amateurism in Sikh art was not anything casual or just phenomenal. It defined the emergence of a new art consciousness where in the artist recreated his own experience to his own vision and to his own delight.

And, it is hence no surprise that the Sikh art which was defined as such only by its sectarian or Sikh theme was not any more as ritual, or conventional as it was before. This recent secular type amateurism had deeply and extensively revolutionalised the Sikh art and its sectarian character. It was not now a thing dictated from outside and executed for a consideration, professional or monetary, or governed and guided by mere religio-conventional compulsions. If anything it was dictated by, it could have been artist's own convictions, aesthetic considerations and need to delight and get delighted. The art now looked at a thing for discovering its ultimate truth and its capacity to delight and move, and sought to interpret life in its own context, and in the contexts of its sufferings and commonality. Sikh art was now the artist's vision of a theme related to Sikh way of life or the Sikh tradition.

Sobha Singh, the known Sikh artist of the 20th century who created his own legends of Sikh Gurus, has given to a series of his portraits of Guru Nanak the title, 'My Meditations on Guru Nanak'. Instead of what the Sikh tradition had so far conceived of Guru Nanak, Sobha Singh's portraits of Guru Nanak represented Sobha Singh's own vision of him. Baba's bearded face blended with Iraqi feminine charm and delicacy, such as Sobha Singh had been caught by for all his life when during the First World War he was in Iraq, underlined Sobha Singh's defiance of the convention. Sobha Singh diluted Baba's Sikhist masculineness adding to it feminine colours. His Nanak's face radiated

139

GURU HAR RAI, THE SEVENTH MASTER
Sikh, Punjab, circa A.D. 1740, Paper, 25 x 16.3 cm, Acc. no: 74.287
Collection: State Museum, Simla, H.P.
The painting is inscribed as—Guru Teg Bahadurji but this inscription seems to be only a later addition wrongly attributing it to Guru Teg Bahadur. The figure of the Guru is seen carrying a walking stick, which only Guru Har Rai is known to have always carried.

(Below left) AN EQUESTRIAN PORTRAIT OF GURU GOBIND SINGH
Guler, Pahari, circa A. D. 1780-1800, Paper, 21.5 x 16.3 cm, Acc. no: F-48
Collection: Govt. Museum and Art Gallery, Chandigarh.

(Below right) AN UNFINISHED PORTRAIT OF GURU GOBIND SINGH
Guler, Pahari, circa A.D. 1800, Paper, 23.5 x 17.8 cm. Acc. no: 57.107/287
Collection: National Museum, New Delhi.

(Opposite page) AN EQUESTRIAN PORTRAIT OF GURU GOBIND SINGH
From Zafar-Namah manuscript, dated 1872 A.D.
Sikh with Guler impact, Punjab, Paper, 30 x 20 cm, Acc. no: M/824
Collection: Patiala Archives, Patiala.

*A set of fine portraits of all ten Sikh Gurus has been rendered at Guler, 1800 A.D., most of which are included in this publication.
Of these the portrait of Guru Gobind Singh alone is equestrian. May be the artist aimed at projecting more powerfully
his saint-warrior personality and his determination to build a stronger community capable of protecting itself and its beliefs
against all oppressions and onslaughts. He has omitted the falcon and halo for he did not want, perhaps,
to attribute his greatness either to any divinity or to a falcon-like instrument of might.
Incidentally this portrait of the Tenth Guru, in all probabilities a work of the known Guler artist Nainsukh,
represents an early phase in the growth of Guruji's portraiture. Though reported from various sources as also from various places,
the five equestrian portraits included in this book grow in a marked way and reveal not only a stylistic continuity
but also an interesting conceptual development. Of this five portraits one is mere drawing meant perhaps for rendering colours later.
The other four have alike spotted horses with their legs and tail –ends painted in orange.
They are alike beautifully saddled and ornamented and all have on their necks yak tails.
With their right side fore- legs lifted they are galloping in an exactly identical style. Guruji's features in all
these portraits are almost alike. He is wearing an alike long jama, almost a similar type of turban,
a bow on his left shoulder and his left hand placed on the bow.*

with a sun-like aura and blushed like lily. He clad him in turban instead his usual *topi* for with halo it has better symmetry and with Sikh tradition, as it grew by artist's own days, greater harmony.

Sohan Singh, another contemporary artist better known as G.S. Sohan Singh, was not the same in his art vision as was his father Giyan Singh, the known *naqqash* of his days. Fine accurate line-work, precision, finish, colour-brilliance, thematic discipline, conventional patterns, models, motifs and strict adherence to 'prescription' characterised his father's commitment to convention. The son believed in revealing the intrinsic aspects of personality, exploring thematic

thrust and probabilities, using abstractions, abstract symbols, better perspective, mysticism, broader and wider contexts.

This shifting of emphasis from a few to all, 'prescription' to innovation, convention to imagination, ritual to secular, professional to amateur, surfacial to intrinsic or mystic, illuminative, illustrative and decorative to explorative, communicative and creative and sensual and sectarian gratification to aesthetic delight and spiritual sublimation was not a phenomenon of art alone, but of the Sikh life as a whole. The transition involved was wider, deeper and all-inclusive, though its intensity was more deeply felt in art the reason being obvious. The indig-

enous art of miniature paintings all over was breathing its last. After the Mughal Empire waned and disintegrated it almost collapsed. Things, however, didn't prove that bad. Pahari, Rajasthani and miniature artists from provinces working at Mughal court shifted to feudatories of the Hills, Rajasthan and Mughal subas who had acclaimed sovereignty and were willing to promote and patronise them. Under their new patrons these artists led the art of miniatures to as great heights as it had attained under Mughals though only for a hundred years or so.

Around the first quarter of the 19th century the decadent phase of the art of Indian miniatures set

GURU GOBIND SINGH'S JOURNEY TO DECCAN
Probably Marwar, Rajasthan, circa A.D. 1770-80
Paper, 51 x 63.5 cm, Collection: S.S.Hitkari, New Delhi.
This painting dominated by Marwar art attributes and with Rajasthani topography
in the background is significant for a typical emblem on the flag and for a Nihang's presence
amidst Guru's five disciples who look like his Panj Piyare.

in once again, and after the 1857 war of Indian people against the British rule failed and the country was fully enslaved to a foreign rule it almost completely collapsed. Mughals, the most sophisticated community representing a great culture rather than a race, religion or rule, had been brutally massacred. After Maharaja Ranjit Singh's death Sikh power had waned and deteriorated. The hill chiefs, already weakened and subordinated to his rule by Maharaja Ranjit Singh, had been rendered further weak and ineffective. The 'formidable' Rajput resistance had lost its force and vigour. All were seen bowing to British in subordination and seeking sustenance in British favour and under their patronage. The British invasion of India was deeper, wider and complete not a grain of resistance against foreign rule surviving. Rajputs were seeking in their life and art capability to appease the British by copying their models or preparing artefacts that suited British taste and decorated the house of British Vice Roy in India and other British buildings. Sikh chiefs, not the common Sikh, so opposed to iconolatry, were creating statue of British emperor George V to be placed at Delhi's India Gate.

British invaders, possessed of a different and strictly their own frame of mind, cultural considerations, art-form, systems of economy, industry, education, administration, civil life, lingual and religious priorities and above all the cult of their own supremacy, had effected a deeper transition in all walks of life of Indian people. The British rule in India was not a mere shifting of political power. It had encroached her entire life putting to subordination all her values, culture, art and thought and shattered and destabilised her entire social structure, economy, industry, customs, creeds, beliefs, traditions and her entire past. They sought to convert India into a British colony in the real sense of the term.

The Pahari artists who had migrated to the Lahore court earlier under Maharaja Ranjit Singh and later under his son Sher Singh, and such artists' descendants struggled for sustaining and preserving the art of Indian miniature and their own Pahari idiom but despite its purity, both as miniature art and Pahari style, was largely lost. It was a complex art scenario, a transition from tenderer themes like *Raga-raginis*, *Baramasa*, love-lores, Krishna-*lila* or Shiva-Parvati anecdotes, myths and legends of past and soft, soothing and colourful natural background of the Himalayan hills to themes of rough and tough war-like life and the flat plains of Punjab. The Pahari art was by and large too delicate to conciliate with such transition. Besides, some

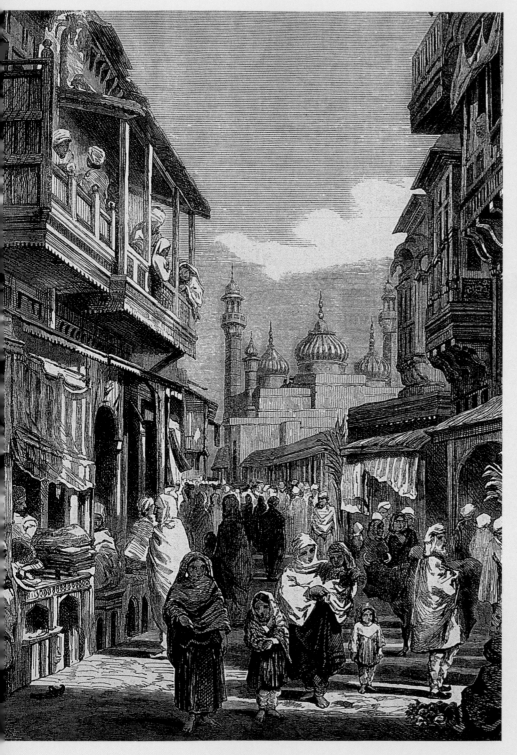

AN ARMY CAMP

*The painting, a combination of landscapic and thematic rendering,
very powerfully depicts an outcamp of the army. the birds seem to be disturbed by the clamour
and noise of the army camp but the elehants and other animals are shown in full leisure.*

(Below left) AKALIS
Sikh, Punjab, Lithograph, late 19th century

(Bottom) COURTIERS OF MAHARAJA RANJIT SINGH
Sikh, Punjab, Paper, mid 19th century
Collection: Hotel Imperial, New Delhi.

(Opposite page right) MIAN MIR, A SUFI SAINT
Sikh, Punjab, Modern, Oil on canvas, 1976, Artist: Gurdit Singh
Collection: Punjab and Sind Bank, New Delhi.

Rajasthani artists migrating to the Lahore court had endowed the art style prevailing at Lahore with attributes of their own art-style, though due to close proximity of the two regions many of the attributes of Rajasthan had long back migrated to Lahore. Thus, in an effort to sustain and preserve the Indian art of miniature in Pahari idiom there evolved at Lahore a subordinate art style comprising of a blend of Pahari and Rajasthani art elements and Sikh theme.

It was incidently the period when several European artists, mainly, Emily Eden, August Schoefft, Baron Hugel, Captain Goldingham, William Carpenter, C.S.Hardinge, and the German painter Von Orlich etc. were at Lahore court as Maharaja's personal guests. The influence they cast on art activities at Lahore was most profound. It revolutionised the total art-scene. Canvas size was now much larger, sometimes looking like a wall-space, with a result that the same theme constituted the subject matter of a fresco as well as a painting on canvas. Broad strokes of the knife instead the usual brush, oil colours instead the vegetable or mineral ones, multi-dimensions, wider and broader perspectives, mysticism, unconventional approach and a wider role of imagination added with minuteness of details, precision, thematic adherence, indigenous motifs and natural back-ground of earlier miniatures defined this later phase of Lahore art, this made Lahore one of the earliest centres of modern art in India and the earliest of modern Sikh art anywhere.

Kehar Singh, besides some artists as Azim, Jeevan Lal and

Hussan-ud-din from Delhi, was the first artist at Lahore accomplished in western style. Kishan Singh, the first Sikh traditionalist, adopted it purely for Sikh themes. Kishan Singh's brother Bishan Singh too worked in western style and on Sikh themes. Bishan Singh's three sons too were artists of good repute and as much devoted to Sikh art, though they worked instead at Amritsar where Sikh art had its second most important centre after Lahore. Raja Ram Kaul Tota, Lahora Singh, Malla Ram who had later shifted to Amritsar, many of his disciples, Hussain Buxe, M.A. Aziz, Sri Ram Lal, Allah Buxe, A.R. Chughtai and Jala-ud-din Chughtai etc., depicting both the Sikh and non-Sikh themes, earned later for Lahore the status of an independent school of modern art. The Punjab love-legends were the more popular themes with these artists and they painted them both on canvas and walls with alike preference.

Sikhism was largely the direction of most of the art activity at Amritsar, Patiala, Chandigarh, Nabha, Jind, Kapurthala etc. Sikh artists painted Sikh themes on very large scale, but their greater contribution consisted in their recreating the past of Punjab. They rendered on canvas and walls the history of Punjab seeking to discover its fresh meaning and relevance, interpreted afresh Sikh legends and conventions and added to Sikh art several new dimensions. Jaswant Singh's symbolic painting of Guru Nanak's life long pilgrimage and travels, by representing just a foot spanning the cosmic background and by a *simarini*, manifested the revolt which the Sikh art had undergone

lately. Jaswant Singh, the artist who conceived this painting, seems to have almost stood up in defiance of the tradition which would not permit a leaf more or less in *Sri Guru Granth Sahib* for it considered the Holy *Granth* as Gurus' body incarnate and could not be hence subjected to any kind of liberty.

Indifferent to convention Jaswant Singh preferred to identify Guru Nanak in his mission, and his mission in an isolated foot traversing the universe, and in a *simarini* symbolising his founding the path of *simaran*. What the rigid convention could have disallowed as distortion, is an excellent piece of symbolic representation. Kirpal Singh, Bodh Raj and Devender Singh are other eminent artists who rendered invaluable service to Sikh art in modern times. Their contribution is of great magnitude and of immense aesthetic and spiritual value. Kirpal Singh and Devender Singh have almost re-created on canvas a Punjab in its totality across its five hundred years. They have recreated in each painting the past of the land. Artistically the fastest movement and rhythm define their lines and forms and make each one of their paintings a great masterpiece.

Large size paintings in Sikh shrines, the Central Sikh Museum, Amritsar, and museums at Anandpur Sahib, Gurdwara Bangla Sahib, Chandigarh, Patiala, Jind, Nabha etc., define the present day idiom of Sikh art. They recreate lives of Sikh Gurus, significant events of the evolution of Sikhism and Sikh history. Stylistically these paintings seem to have evolved out of Bazar-art combined with the elements of Pahari, Rajasthani and Company art styles developed at Lahore and used widely for embellishing theatrical auditoriums. Despite largely influenced by such blend of art styles the Sikh artists, as is evident from their painted works, followed only the modern masters like Ravi Verma, Nand Lal Bose and Abinindra Nath Tagore etc. Visual element dominates these paintings, though such visual elements have been included aiming at inspiring in common mind the feelings of piety, splendour, devotion and reverence for the great Sikh tradition.

Lithographs engraved from the works of earlier masters like Emily Eden, William Carpenter etc., copies of the works of such masters, calender art, textiles, ivory, glass and other art media played a vital role in the growth of Sikh art. Hotel Imperial, New Delhi and Maharaja Ranjit Singh Museum, Amritsar, have in their collection a number of outstanding lithographs of great antique value. The Punjab & Sind Bank, New Delhi's collection of modern Sikh paintings is alike invaluable.

S.S. Hitkari, a private collector of antiquities, has in his collection invaluable paintings, both the medieval and modern, *Phulkaris* and *Bagh* and other textiles, and several other artefacts. These invaluable treasures define the great Sikh art and the heritage of a great community, religious thought and culture.

The Sikh heritage, far more than a mere system of thought, rituals, worship or a way of *His* realisation, manifests in life's totality, in its faith, thought and practices, sanctions and prohibitions, customs and costumes, industry and endeavour, aspirations and containability, freedom and restraints, individual living, social relations, community life, architecture and building structures, kind of food, working habits, education patterns, trades, textiles, artefacts, items of day-to-day use, art, culture, traditions, conventions, rituals, language and literature, and all that relates to life. War is its aspect and so is peace. Renunciation might be an element foreign to it but the house-hold constitutes its very core. The entire Punjab, its land and sky, vibrates with Sikhism, a spiritual legacy of Guru Nanak, strengthened by other Sikh Gurus and given its final shape and character by the Tenth and the last personal Guru, Guru Gobind Singh.

(Previous pages) MY MEDITATIONS ON GURU NANAK
Sikh, Punjab, Modern, Oil on canvas
Artist: Sobha Singh
Collection: Govt. Museum and Art Gallery, Chandigarh.

GURU NANAK, THE PILGRIM
Sikh, Punjab, Modern, Oil on canvas
Artist: Jaswant Singh, Acc. no: 3311
Collection: Govt. Museum and Art Gallery, Chandigarh.
Hai kahan tamanna ka dusara kadam yarab,
Hamne daste-imkan ko ek nakshe pa paya
This painting is an excellent example of abstract symbolism where in a foot and
simarini portray Baba Nanak's life devoted to his mission with which he traverse
the entire land and his path of Nam-Simran.

Aspects of Great Importance

Sikh Numismatics
G.S. Cheema

The coinage of Lahore *Durbar* and the prior anarchic republic of the *Dal Khalsa*, possessed of features characteristically its own, distinguishing it from the contemporary Mughal, post-Mughal and Durrani coinage, constitutes a separate class of numismatics to name essentially as the Sikh. A Sikh coin, with nothing to distinguish the one struck by Maharaja Ranjit Singh from the other by Maharaja Sher Singh or Duleep Singh, is never a ruler's coin, as are the contemporary Mughal or Durrani coins attributed to one *Badshah* or the other. An adherence to Sikhism by way of inclusion of some venerable Sikh motifs and a complete absence of any reference to an earthly ruler or *Badshah* distinguishes a coin as Sikh. A Sikh coin's *Badshah* is always and in all cases only the *Sachcha Patshah*, the Guru. As such, the coins that evolved under Sikh rulers acquired a Sikh character, giving them an identity different from other classes of numismatics and earning for themselves a distinct name.

The ruler's name on a coin, on obverse or reverse, has always and all over been, (save in modern democratic rule), an essentiality of numismatic conceptualisation. The coins struck by Sikh rulers,

GOLD *MOHAR* OF MAHARAJA RANJIT SINGH
Dia: 2 cm, wt: 10.8 gms, Acc. no: 65.496
Collection: National Museum, New Delhi.
Obverse: Guru Gobind Singh and Fazl,
Legend: Sikka zad bar har do alam
Reverse: Vikram Samvat-1863, A.D. 1806
Mint: Amritsar 'Sri Amrit…' partially readable.

by abstaining from mentioning the names of them who issued them, mark a characteristic departure. Instead in the name of any individual ruler, the coins of Banda Bahadur, Maharaja Ranjit Singh, Sher Singh, Duleep Singh and others were issued in Sikh Gurus' names, especially the first and the last. Thus, giving such coins a puritanical fervour of Sikh faith. To Sikh rulers, The Gurus alone were *Sachcha Patshahs*, the true kings, and the rest mere dross as compared to genuine ones. The *Kalima* of the contemporary Mughal coins or Persian verses of other coins mentioning *Badshah's* names were replaced in the coins of Sikh rulers with appropriate inscriptions praising their Gurus, Baba Nanak and Guru Gobind Singh in particular.

This self-imposed discipline of early Sikh rulers later became for succeeding ones a sectarian commandment and for Sikh coins an acclaimed standard. Sardar Jassa Singh of the Ahluwalia Misl who issued a coin with a two-line distich containing his own name on its obverse after he occupied Lahore for a brief span in 1761, was perhaps the only one to stray from the precedence. This impertinence of Sardar Jassa Singh was aptly dealt with in the next *Sarbat Khalsa*. He was reportedly admonished and the coins were recalled. Not many of the Sikh coins have been preserved and brought to light. This coin of Sardar Jassa Singh is amongst such unavailable ones, though Mr. Brown claims to have seen some of them. The story relating to his admonition may be thus apocryphal.

The coins of all other Sikh rulers reported from various sources adhere to this precedence. Banda Bahadur is said to have struck coins from mint described as the *zinat-ul-takhta Mubarak bakhta-i-Khalsa* and *muswarat shahar ba aman-ul-dahr*, that is: the city of counsel, the refuge of the age, the glory of the throne of the *Khalsa*, and the one who bestows eternal peace. For long these coins too were known only from Kamwar Khan's *Taz kirat-us-Salatin-i-Chughataiya*, and only three specimens of this coin have been reported in the duration of past thirty-three years. As reported, its obverse legend is as follows:

Sikka zad bar har do alam,
tegh-i-Nanak wahab ast,
Fateh Gobind Shah-i-Shahan,
fazi-i- Sacha Sahib ast

(Coin struck in both the worlds; the sword of Nanak is the bestower; by the grace of true Lord, the victory is Gobind's, King of Kings). The more commonly found subsequent coins issued by the Amritsar and Lahore mints later present some variants of this legend.

An ordinary Lahore mint imperial coin bearing the name of Shah Alam, the Mughal emperor ruling as Bahadur Shah I, and of

(Above left) A COIN STAMPER STAMPING A RUPEE
The inscription on the top border is as: 'Rupaye par Mohar si kaiskari lagada hay'.

(Above right) A MINT *(TAKSAL)*
The inscription on top border is: 'Sahib yar taksal kacha sarkaunda hay',
Some sahib Yar is inspecting a mint.

Sikh, Patiala, Punjab, late 19th century, Paper, 27.5 x 21.5 cm, Acc. no: 88.340, 342
Collection: National Museum, New Delhi.

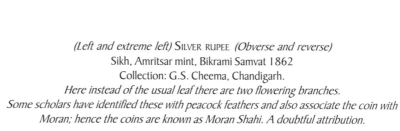

the period when Banda Bahadur took up the role of the scourge of God and set the Punjab on fire, is another coin, and a queer one to have been associated with this champion of Sikh cause. It contains quite unbelievably, on its obverse flan a curious symbol bearing a remarkable resemblance to the *Khalsa* emblem of crossed swords, *Khanda* and *chakra*. The resemblance is too uncanny to be a mere coincidence. Maybe, after Banda Bahadur's emergence, the erstwhile Mughal coins of Shah Alam were hurriedly converted on Sikh lines to serve the immediate purpose of this Sikh ruler.

The first Sikh coins were issued from Lahore, the traditional seat of power, the *Dar-ul-Sultanat*, as it was described in the Mughal coinage, instead of Amritsar. Sikhs had occupied Lahore in 1765, the greater part being held by the *Bhangi Sardars with Kanhaiyas* in the south. The inscription that the obverse flan of these coins reads as follows:

Degh, tegh-o-fateh,
o nusrat-i-bedrang
Yaft az Nanak Guru Gobind
Singh

(From Nanak Guru Gobind Singh acquired the willingness to share, the sword (of righteousness), the certainty of victory, and promptness in offering

assistance).The reverse inscription, oddly enough, followed the old Mughal formula, namely, *Jalus, Maimnat, Manus, Zarb Dar ul Sultanat Lahore*, with the difference that herein was used *Vikrami samvat*. The distich in the later coins changed to :

Sikka zad bar seem o zar fazl
Sacha Sahib ast, Fateh Gobind
Singh Shah-i-Shahan,
Tegh-i-Nanak wahab ast

(Coin in gold and silver was struck by the Grace of the True Lord. The victory is Gobind Singh's, the King of Kings, by the grace of Nanak). Later they incorporated the familiar leaf symbol constantly used then onwards, though with variations in shape. The first Amritsar mint coins are dated *Samvat* 1832(1778 A.D.). The legend on their obverse varies a little:

Sikka zad bar har do alam fazl
Sacha Sahib ast,
Fateh tegh Guru Gobind Singh
Shah Nanak wahib ast

(Coin was struck for two worlds by the grace of True Lord, victory to the sword of Guru Gobind Singh, by the grace of Shah Nanak). The mint is described as *Zarb Sri*

Amritsar Ji-o, bakhta Akal Takht. That is, mint *Sri Amritsar ji-o*, by the grace of *Akal Takht*— the Timeless Throne. The obverse legend went on varying but the mention of the *Akal Takht* was ever constant.

With the assumption of the sole authority after the seizure of Lahore in 1799, Maharaja Ranjit Singh was a force to reckon with. However he, too, preferred not to deviate from the standards set for the Sikh coinage. It seems, he was aware of Sikhs' strong republican character and of the fact that an overt insistence on monarchical authority would only work against him. He knew that he could be supreme as long as the fiction of the sovereignty of the *Sacha Sahib* worked. Hence, his coins were more or less a continuity of prior Sikh coin concept.

The dates of many coins vary from a frozen to a possibly true one and sometimes both. The leaf symbol is sometimes replaced by an *arsi*, a small circular hand mirror associated with courtesans. On 'Moran' rupee (named after Mora, a favourite courtesan of Maharaja Ranjit Singh) the leaf symbol is replaced by a twin spray of leaves. Though the leaf symbol was more or less constant, variants like *katar*, *trishul*, and *swastika* and flag, were seen occurring on later coins struck by local powers. Thus the illuminative or decorative aspect of coins related to Sikh rulers went on changing. Yet such coins' adher-

ence to Sikh faith and Gurus' sovereignty was always the same.

There are some other curious aspects of Sikh numismatics. The coins of Najibabad mint carry on one flan the symbols and legends pertaining to Rohilla issues whereas on the other the standard Sikh legend of the Amritsar mint. Such a scheme is repeated on coins from Jaipur mint. It seems Jaipur mint coins were struck by some raider as the inscription, *Urdu zafar qarin* (that is, the auspicious and victorious camp) on such coins suggests. Maybe, Sikhs had, like great Mughals, their ambulant mint to accompany them when they were on move for some longer duration.

Most strange and unfortunate is the case of Sikh states of the Cis-Sutlej region. But for Nabha, which followed the usual pattern prevailing in trans-Sutlej states, Patiala, Jind and Kaithal carried on their coins fragments of the Durrani legend. Instead of a mention of Sikh Gurus, their coins contained the name of Ahmed Shah Durrani who shed more Sikh blood than any Mughal or any other invader. Not only that, Patiala rulers accepted commission, titles and other favours from Ahmed Shah Durrani or retained

along with the rulers of Kaithal, Jind and Malerkotla the abhorrent Sirhind as their mint name. They also acclaimed on their coins Ahmed Shah Durrani as representing the Almighty indirectly disowning their own Gurus and got inscribed on them cryptic figure of 4 considered auspicious in Islamic tradition. The couplet their coins contained read as follows:

*Sikka zad bar sim wa zar az auj
mahi bamah
Hukm shud az qadir bechun ba
Ahmad badshah*

(That is, coins in silver and gold Ahmad Badshah struck on the command of the Almighty from the earth to the moon).

The believing or superstitious mind might say that such disregard to the Gurus would counterly work and it did. These states could mint their own coins but they stooped to the level of what today be called 'non-circulating legal tender'. The coins these states struck were ac-

ceptable only within the peripheries of these states and were mere metal pieces outside. Their circulation was soon restricted to ceremonial or formal use.

The coins of Lahore *Durbar* and of the *Dal Khalsa* that preceded it are remarkable for their fine calligraphy, which contrasts strongly with the often-barbaric fabric of the contemporary Mughal coinage of shadowy emperors like Ahmad, Alamgir II and the early Shah Alam II. The gold and silver coins of the Lahore *Durbar* and the *Dal Khalsa*, almost without exception, carry Persian legends. The *Gurmukhi* characters seem to have been used only for copper coins and, like most of other contemporary non-Sikh coins, are crude and barbaric minted in all probabilities by private agencies. The gold and silver coinage of the later Sadozais, particularly Mahmud Shah and Shuja-ul-Mulk is more attractive with calligraphy almost superb. And, it seems the Sadozais coins borrowed this finesse from Sikh coins of Lahore *Durbar* and of the *Dal Khalsa* instead from those of their own predecessors. Thus, whosoever the rulers, the Sikh tradition cast its deep impact on coinage of a large part of northern and central India.

The Golden Temple

◆

Dr. Mohinder Singh

The Golden Temple has been from its very inception the spiritual as well as the temporal center of the Sikh world. The significance of the place where the Temple stands is variedly sought from pre-historic days to Sikh Guru's own times. As goes the tradition, the Amritsar, nectar-reservoir, the site where the fourth Sikh Guru Ram Das founded his holy city, was in existence much before *Ramavatara*. Rama's predecessor, Iksvaka, is alluded to have performed a great *yajna* here. The site's nectaral significance was rediscovered when Guru Angad's skin disease was cured with a herb discovered existing here. The husband of Rajni, the daughter of Rai Duni Chand who suffered from leprosy was cured with a dip into nectaral water of Amritsar. May be, Guru Ram Das chose the site for its great medicinal properties.

The holy city was initially laid as Chak Ram Dass. Its land was donated to Bibi Bhani, consort of Guru Ram Das, by the Mughal emperor Akbar who, while returning from Rajasthan, halted at Guru's *langar* and was highly impressed

with this community kitchen. He wanted to gift the Guru a *jagir* but on his declining the offer, donated to his wife this piece of land. As per another version, the said land was bought for Rupees seven hundred from *zamindars* of village Tung by Guru Ram Das himself. The *sar* or tank, was developed by *karsewa*, devotees' free service.

The construction of the temple, initially Hari Mandir, in the center of the tank was carried out by fifth Guru Arjan Dev. In consultation with Baba Buddhaji, a veteran senior Sikh, Guruji himself conceived its design. In the spirit of Sikh tradition of religious tolerance, its foundation was laid by a Muslim divine, Mian Mir. Again in keeping with Sikh spirit of humility the temple was laid on a low plinth. It was conceived with four openings on all four sides symbolising its accessibility to all four varnas of Indian society. The main access was provided across a causeway leading to the main gate *Darshani Deorhi*. The construction was carried out mainly by Sikhs under Guru's own supervision and with contributions received from devout. After the temple was com-

pleted Guru Arjan Dev composed a hymn thanking Almighty for it. Later the sacred *Adi-granth*, after Guru Arjan Dev had compiled it, was consecrated in the Temple in a grand ceremony. The temple was now an abode of Him whom Sikh Gurus had realised in their *Bani*. This permanent repository of *Gurbani*, the *Adi-granth* to be revered later as *Sri Guru Granth Sahib*, was Gurus' body visible.

The Golden Temple, with its own distinction amongst Indian shrines, has a simple, puritan yet highly elegant unique architecture. Its initial design is now a matter of only guess for it was often attacked and demolished by Islamic invaders and underwent renovation or reconstruction as often. Golden Temple's architectural form, as it persists today, save its gold plating and embellishment, seems to be a continuity of the form arrived at during its reconstruction, pursuing perhaps its prior architectural plan, carried out by confederation of Sikh misldars under Sardar Jassa Singh Ramgarhia after Ahmad Shah Abdali's attack in 1765. Later the temple's exterior was gold plated and interior decorated with carvings and painted panels by Maharaja Ranjit Singh, which gave the temple its Swarn Mandir name. The carving was accomplished by expert Muslim and murals by Pahari artists. The Temple's main entrance records 'the Guru was kind enough to allow the privilege of service to the temple to his humble servant Ranjit Singh'.

The main body of the temple rises from a 150m square base in the middle of the tank. The causeway, a 60m long passage connecting with *Darshani Deorhi*, is bordered with balustrades of fretted marble intercepted by lampposts of marble columns containing huge lanterns. On its base the Harmandir Sahib has a 52m square plinth. The lower part of the Temple consists of white marble and upper plated with gold. The interior, a central space and circumbulatory around defined by magnificently embellished huge columns, houses lavishly decorated and jewels studded canopy under which has been consecrated *Sri Guru Granth Sahib*. This interior is single storied rising from floor level to temple's apex which consists of a roof surmounted by a small pavilion with fluted golden dome, four corner kiosks and a line of seven copper clad parapet ting domes on each four sides and gold *chhatra*.

The vaulted ceiling over the canopy has been embellished with designs in gold and is studded with precious and semi-precious stones, jewels and mirrors. On mid height over the circumbulatory there is a large projected balcony with all its interior studded with decorative mirrors and murals giving the impression of an independent floor. It has five magnificently decorated openings on each side overlooking the main central hall installing the sacred canopy. This overhung floor inlaid in variedly patterned reflecting pieces of glass, along a similar gilded and inlaid ceiling is sometimes called the *Sheesh Mahal*. On its east the prior square structure has been now appended with a semi-hexagonal building giving the temple a hexagon-square shape. The walls from ground level are carried along several beautifully rounded pinnacles. The beauty, perspectives of height and magnificence of the temple are many times multiplied when this gold mound reflect in the waters of the sacred tank.

A recent photograph of Golden Temple, Amritsar.
(Opposite page) A painting of Golden Temple on ivory

Phulkaris: The Embroidered Dreams of Punjab

◆

S.S Hitkari

Phulkari, the word meaning flower work, was first used in Waris Shah's famous folk tale *Heer Ranjha*. The word has its root in Irani *gulkari*. In India the *'gul'* was replaced by *'phul'*. During Maharaja Ranjit Singh's reign, *phulkari* gained immense popularity as a craft. Initially, the *phulkari* was a coarse home-spun *khaddar*, which Punjab women embroidered with *pat*, a silk thread, in simple stitches called *darn*. *Phulkari* involved a kind of afternoon socialising, the *trinjan*, when the women folk, after their day's work was over, gathered and engaged in deft embroidery or knitting. It was in the first quarter of the 19th century that the *phulkari* became an item of adornment.

Phulkaris, an art tradition handed down from mother to daughter, were used for marriages and other joyous occasions. A significant part of a girl's dowry included *phulkaris*, consisting of 21 to 101 *baghs*, a richer type of *phulkari*. Women were honoured with *bagh* and *phulkaris* soon after childbirth, as also before they resumed normal household chores. *Phulkari* draped the coffin of a *suhagan* the woman who died in her husband's lifetime. Connected intimately with all significant stages of a woman's life made *phulkari* a labour of love. Initially *phulkaris* were rarely

PULKARI
Sikh, Punjab, 19th century, cotton and silk thread, 2.5 x 1.5 m
Collection: S.S. Hitkari, New Delhi.
This pulkari is considered as one of the rarest and known as
Bawan (52) pulkari. There are fifty two different patterns embroidered in each box.

bought or sold, nor they enjoy any significant patronage. It was a mother's pious duty to prepare needed ones for her daughter or daughter-in-law with her own hands and was thus a folk art in its truest sense.

Sparsely embroidered floral and geometrical motifs characterised early *phulkari*. Later when embroidery covered the entire surface of the base cloth *phulkaris* came to be known as *bagh*, literally, the 'garden', something consuming good labour and time. Perfect design symmetry is achieved by embroidering from the wrong side of the cloth and by carefully counting each and every stitch.

The *phulkaris* and *baghs* of eastern and western Punjab have stylistic difference. The western population was urbanized and affluent, hence both the base and the floss silk used there were fine and expensive. The base colour was usually a tint of red for younger women and white for elderly ones. Black and blue were prohibited. Silken floss was usually in white, yellow or pale orange like soft tints. The designs were geometrical. Figures were not in use. The workmanship was exceptionally sophisticated. With meager Hindus and Sikhs population, the production of *phulkaris* in this part was proportionately lower. Much of the lot was destroyed in the post-partition riots, and as

much was left behind. Now older *phulkaris* and *baghs* from western Punjab are a rarity.

Phulkaris from east Punjab are more readily available. They make use of various shades of red and sometimes black and blue but white only exceptionally. The colours of the *pat* are rich and vibrant and *pallus* heavily embroidered. The motifs were derived from day-today life. These *baghs* derived their names like *Chand, sheesh, lehariya, kanki, motia, mor, mirchi bagh* from the motifs like moon, mirror, waves, wheat, jasmine, peacock and chilli that dominated them.

Phulkaris continue to dominate various ceremonial occasions and get named accordingly. The *chope* is a wedding *phulkari*, a longer one in size whose open ended border-less length symbolizes long happy marital life. It is offered to the bride by her maternal uncle immediately before the actual wedding takes place. The base is always in red, the colour of passion, love and union, and embroidery is done in yellow, which ensures prosperity and fertility. Primary motifs are two triangles. They have their bases towards either end of the base cloth and apex towards center. They represent male and female principles and the space between their apex the unconsummated state of marriage.

When marriage rites including

circumambulating *Sri Guru Granth Sahib* take place a bride is required to wear *suber phulkari*, known to have five six-petalled lotus flowers, four on corners and one in center. They symbolise beauty, purity and goodness. Six petals formed of two triangles symbolise by multiplication stronger unity in married life. A profusion of such flowers, with four larger ones on corners, images of gods and those of couple's ancestors on margins mark the *suber phulkaris*.

Bawan baghs is a rarer type of *phulkari*. It consists of fifty two, i.e., *bawan* designing patterns on a single piece of cloth. The *sainchi phulkaris*, embroidered only in Bhatinda and Moga districts are another distinguished kind of *phulkaris*. They usually depict folklores, customs, flora and fauna of the region. A woman plying spinning wheel, churning curd or carrying meals to her farmer husband, *chaupar* playing males, *madaris* with monkeys and bears, wrestlers, acrobats, Lord Krishna with *gopis*, Hanuman, birds, animals and insects are their common motifs.

Phulkaris have great cultural significance and are Punjab's such characteristic art form that all handicraft emporiums of Punjab, anywhere in India and abroad, bear 'Phulkari' as their name. If any single craft defines Punjab it is *phulkari*.

159

A FIGURATIVE *PULKARI*
Sikh, Punjab, early 20th century, cotton and silk thread, 2.5 x 1.5 m
Collection: S.S. Hitkari, New Delhi.
This pulkari is known, as 'Sainchi' There are various scenes depicting daily life of the villagers, flora and fauna found in the villages, sports, spinning and several other village scenes.

Shawls: A Manifestation of Sikh Life Texture

◆

Anamika Pathak

SHAWL
Woven Pashmina and hand embroidered
Kashmir style at Amritsar, end of 19th century
10 ft 2" x 4 ft 4", Acc. no: 56.41/5
Collection: National Museum, New Delhi.

The shawls, an artefact usually associated with Kashmir for its origin, more than a piece of mere textile or drapery, belong to the realm of arts sharing Kashmir's delicacy, refinement, and skill of its people. The Kashmir shawls attained great qualitative and quantitative heights, expansion and market beyond the valley and India, a jewel like status, new forms and other characters and came in common man's reach under Sikh patronage. This shawls' model is usually defined as Kashmiri Sikh shawls.

These shawls and prior Kashmiri ones were *Kanikar* (woven) and *amlikar* (embroidered). The Sikh art motifs and features emerged into these shawls after Maharaja Ranjit Singh captured Lahore. Artists, after the Mughal Empire weakened, migrated from Delhi to Lahore where under Maharaja Ranjit Singh they found a great patron, most congenial art climate and best alternative. He had a natural preference for themes and art motifs which reflected Sikh faith and wished to see them in various artefacts but due to his weakness for shawls more particularly in them. This revolutionized the production of shawls and quality of their embellishment.

A shawl was an essential part of the costumes of Maharaja Ranjit Singh and his nobles. Several con-

temporary paintings including the British Museum's miniature depicting 'the death of Maharaja Ranjit Singh' underline the importance of shawls in the Sikh world of Maharaja Ranjit Singh. This miniature depicts three shawls, one yellow under his dead body, a maroon over it, and a third striped jamawar lying pillow-like under his head.

The Sikh shawls are larger in size. The shawls, falling under the category of 'classical', continued with prior designing patterns, others, classed as ' modern', marked a departure from them. The classical type of shawls consisted of both, the plain *matan* (field) with *kalka botehs* and the *matan* decorated all over. Embroidered shawls were more popular and costlier. The National Museum, New Delhi has both kinds of shawls. Its plain *matan* shawl of circa 1825-30 woven with fine wool in cream colour, comprising of *kalka botehs*, *dhor* (running ornament surrounding the field), *tanjir* (lateral border ornament), *palla* (large patterned border at each end) and *hashiya* (border) is a precious piece of this period. *Palla* comprises of eight *kalka botehs* set in between patterns such as cypress trees, lotus type roses or fool's cap, blue tiny flowers and greenish-gray floral creepers etc. The same pattern is repeated in *dhor* and corner *botehs*, which are embroidered, not woven. The upper-most portion consists of stylized floral creepers and the *tanjir* and *hashiya* of winding hooked vine and lotus type roses all over, balancing in great perfection the main motif and *hashiya* pattern. Colours' choice, design, pattern and size are characteristically Sikhist.

The shawls on Sikh themes falling under the category of modern were more stylistic. Tapestry shawls, a new class, depicting a theme with an underlying abstract symbolism, were created under the modern school. The National Museum has in its collection a fine tapestry shawl. Colourful, large sized, long end panels, *tanjir*, *dhor*, small central *matan* and *hashiya* characterise this shawl. Its long end panel illustrates sweeping *botehs*, spandrel pattern, cypress tree motifs, and on the upper portion shrine like decoration surrounded by a pair of peacocks, flowers and a row of cypresses arranged in garden style. These patterns are rendered in green, maroon, yellow, pink and blue.

The small sized square woolen shawls containing usually four semi-circles on corners and a full circle in the center, all on a plain ground, known as *chandar* or moon shawls, also underwent a drastic change. Now their size was larger, square format, rectangular and the plain ground decked with Sikhist designs. A moon shawl consisting of two or four separately woven panels joined together with great precision to form a square in its middle was an innovation of this period. The Sikh influence is also perceivable in abstract images and incorporated in these shawls, the oriental culture. A highly fascinating transition adopting symbolic contents.

Amli shawls had an earlier beginning, but they too gained popularity during the Sikh period. *Amli* shawls took little time to get popular for they had several advantages over a *kani* shawl. They saved time, skill and cost. It was actually the *amli* shawls that gave to Punjab the status of a shawl manufacturing region and to Amritsar of the best center for washing, dying, fringe and border setting. As early as 1834, Amritsar had become come a major center for *Amli* shawls. It is said that Maharaja Ranjit Singh had commissioned embroiderers to manufacture a pair of shawls depicting his victories. It seems the later figurative Kashmir map shawls grew out of them, though only four of them were reported from various museums.

Under Sikhs, changes that occurred in terms of size, design, colour, motifs, kind of fabrics and in entire tradition, added altogether new and indigenous dimensions to the shawl industry and opened new horizons giving shawls a global geography. Hence, today Punjab is the biggest manufacturer and largest seller of so-called Kashmir shawls in India.

WOVEN PASHMINA SHAWL
Kashmir style at Amritsar, end of 19th century
11 ft 3" x 5 ft", Acc. no: 61.8
Collection: National Museum, New Delhi.

Bibliography

1.	Aijazuddin, F.S.	: Pahari painting and Sikh portraits in the Lahore Museum, London, 1977.
2.	——Do——	: Sikh portraits by European artists, London, 1977.
3.	Allen, Marguerite	: The Golden Lotus of Amritsar, Calcutta 1955.
4.	Ahuja, Dr.Roshan Lal	: Maharaja Ranjit Singh–A Man of Destiny, New Delhi, 1983.
5.	Anand, Mulk Raj	: Marg vol.x, no.2, [ed] Bombay, March 1957 & vol. viii, no xxx, 1977.
6.	——Do——	: Maharaja Ranjit Singh as patron of the arts, Bombay [Marg] 1981.
7.	——Do——	: Golden Temple, Marg [ed.] 1977.
8.	Archer, W.G.	: Painting of the Sikhs, London, 1965.
9.	——Do——	: Indian Painting in the Punjab Hills, London, 1973.
10.	Aryan, K.C.	: Punjab Painting, Patiala, 1975.
11.	——Do——	: Punjab Murals, New Delhi, 1977.
12.	Ashok, Shamsher Singh	: Sri Darbar Sahib, Tarn Taran, Amritsar.
13.	—Do——	: Itihas Gurdwara Sahib, Muktsar, Amritsar, 1971.
14.	—Do——	: Nishan-te-Hukum-Name, Punjabi, [ed.], Amritsar, 1967.
15.	Bajwa, Fauja Singh	: The military system of the Sikhs during the period 1799 -1849, Delhi.
16.	Banerjee, Indubhushan	: Evolution of the Khalsa, 2 vols. Calcutta, 1972.
17.	Berinstain, V.	: Phulkari embroidered flowers from Punjab, Punjab, Paris.
18.	Bhai Vir Singh	: Varan Bhai Gurdas [ed. Punjabi text] 1951.
19.	Brown, Kerry	: Sikh art and literature [ed.] London, 1999.
20.	Col, W.O. and Sambhi, P.S.	: Sikhs, their Beliefs and Practices, London, 1978.
21.	Cunningham, J.A.	: History of the Sikhs, from the origins of the Nation to the battles of the Satluj, London, 1849.
22.	Daljeet, Dr.	: Mughal and Deccani Painting [from the collection of the National Museum], New Delhi, 1999.
23.	——Do——	: Guru Nanak — A Portfolio, New Delhi, 1998.
24.	——Do——	: Guru Gobind Singh — A Portfolio, New Delhi, 1999.
25.	Eden, Emily	: Up the country Letters from India, London, 1844, Reprint 1978.
26.	Goswamy, B.N.	: Painters at the Sikh court: a study based on Twenty documents, Wiesbaden, 1975.
27.	——Do——	: Essence of Indian art, Sanfrancisco, 1986.
28.	——Do——	: Piety and Splendour, Sikh Heritage in Art, New Delhi, 2000.
29.	Goswamy, B.N. and Fischer Eberhard	: Pahari Masters- Court painters of Northern India, Zurich, 1997.
30.	Goswamy, Karuna	: Frescoes in the Sheesh Mahal at Patiala, Roop-Lekha, and vol.38 No.1-2 All India Fine Arts and Crafts Society, New Delhi.
31.	——Do——	: Kashmiri Painting: Assimilation and Diffusion; Production and Patronage, Simla, 1998.
32.	Grewal, J.S.	: The Sikhs of the Punjab, 1990.
33.	——Do——	: Guru Nanak in History, Chandigarh, 1969.
34.	Gupta, Hari Ram	: A History of the Sikhs, 3 vols. Lahore and Simla, 1944 -1952.
35.	Gupta, P.L.	: The coins of the Dal Khalsa and Lahore Darbar, Chandigarh, 1989.

36. Gupta, S.N.   : The Sikh School of Painting, Rupam, vol. 3 no.12.

37. Hans. Herrli   : The coins of the Sikhs, Nagpur, 1993.

38. Hans. Surjeet   : The B-40 Janamsakhi, (ed.) Amritsar, 1987.

39. Howarth, Stephen   : The Koh-i-Noor diamond: the History and the Legend, London, 1980.

40. Irwin, J.   : The Kashmir shawl, London, 1973.

41. Johar, Surinder Singh   : Hand Book on Sikhism, Delhi, 1977.

42. ——Do——   : The Sikh Gurus and their Shrines, Delhi, 1976.

43. Kang, Kanwaljit Singh   : Wall Paintings of Punjab, 1979.

44. ——Do——   : Wall Paintings of Punjab and Haryana, New Delhi, 1985.

45. Kaur, Madanjeet   : The Golden Temple: Past and Present, Amritsar, 1983.

46. ——Do——   : Painter of the Divine — Sobha Singh, Amritsar, 1987.

47. Khandalavala, Karl J.   : Pahari Miniature Painting, Bombay, 1958.

48. Latif, S.M.   : History of the Punjab, Reprint, New Delhi, 1964.

49. Losty, Jeremiah P.   : The Art of the Book in India, London, 1982.

50. McLeod, W.H.   : Guru Nanak and the Sikh Religion, Delhi, 1968.

51. ——Do——   : Textual Sources for the Study of Sikhism, Manchester, 1984.

52. ——Do——   : The B-40 Janamsakhi, [translated and Ed.] Amritsar, 1980.

53. ——Do——   : Early Sikh Tradition: A Study of the Janamsakhis, Oxford, 1980.

54. ——Do——   : Popular Sikh Art, Delhi, 1991.

55. Pant, G.N.   : Indian Arms and Armour, 3 vols. New Delhi, 1978.

56. Paul, Suwarcha   : Sikh Miniatures in the Chandigarh Museum, Chandigarh, 1985.

57. Randhawa, M.S.   : Sikh Paintings, Rooplekha, vol. 39 no 1.

58. ——Do——   : "Kehar Singh and Kapur Singh: Two Punjabi Artists of the 19th century", Chhavi, vol. I.

59. ——Do——   : Kangra Ragamala Painting, New Delhi.

60. Randhawa, T.S.   : The Sikh Images, New Delhi, 2000

61. Singh, Patwant   : The Golden Temple, New Delhi, 1988.

62. Singh, Harbans   : Encyclopaedia of Sikhism, 4 vols. Patiala, 1992-99.

63. Singh, Khuswant   : A History of the Sikhs, Delhi, 1991.

64. ——Do——   : Maharaja Ranjit Singh, Maharaja of the Punjab, London, 1962.

65. ——Do——   : Japjee, Sikh Morning Prayer (translated) New Delhi, 1999.

66. Singh, Dr. Mohinder   : The Golden Temple, Hongkong, 1994.

67. Singh, Fauja and Arora, A.C.   : Maharaja Ranjit Singh, Politics, Society and Economy, Patiala, 1984(edited).

68. Singh, Kirpal   : The Historical Study of Maharaja Ranjit Singh's Times, New Delhi, 1994.

69. Singh, Teja and Ganda Singh   : A Short History of the Sikhs, Bombay, 1950.

70. Stronge, Susan   : The Arts of the Sikh Kingdoms (ed.) London, 1999.

71. Srivastava, R.P.   : Punjab Painting, New Delhi, 1990.

72. Srivastava, S.P.   : Art and Cultural Heritage of Patiala, New Delhi, 1983.

73. Waheeduddin, Fakir Syed   : The Real Ranjit Singh, Karachi, 1965.

74. Welch, Stuart C.   : India, Art and Culture, 1300-1900, New York, 1985.

Acknowledgements

ANANDPUR SAHIB FOUNDATION
Chairman and all the members of the Executive Committee of the Anandpur Sahib Foundation.
Shri Gurjeet Singh Cheema, Principle Secretary, Culture, Government of Punjab.
Smt. Vini Mahajan, Chief Executive Officer, Anandpur Sahib Foundation, Chandigarh.
Shri P.S. Bhopal, Nodel Officer, and all the staff members of Anandpur Sahib Foundation.

DEPARTMENT OF CULTURE, GOVT. OF PUNJAB, CHANDIGARH
Shri Inderjit Singh Sandhu, Director
Shri Gurdev Singh, Senior Technical Assistant
Shri K.K. Rishi, Archaeological Officer
Smt. Parminder Kaur, Assistant Archivist
Shri Raman Kumar, Assistant Curator
Shri Lakhvinder Singh Sodhi, Curator
Shri Kuldeep Singh, Senior Technical Assistant
Shri Baldev Singh
Shri Jaswant Singh, Art Executive
Smt. Arvind Kaur and all the staff members of the Department of Culture.

GOVT. MUSEUM AND ART GALLERY, CHANDIGARH
Shri V. N. Singh, Director
Smt. Poonam Khanna, Curator

NATIONAL MUSEUM, NEW DELHI
Dr. R.D. Chowdhary, Director General
Shri U. Das, Assistant Director

Dr. Vijay Kumar Mathur, Museum Education Officer
Shri S.P. Singh, Chief Restorer
Smt. Pratibha Parashar, Library and Information Officer
Shri K.K.Gupta, Senior Restorer
Smt. Anamika Pathak, Deputy Keeper
Shri B.L. Anand, Kishan Lal and Raghav Manjhi

PHOTOGRAPHERS
Shri Rajbir Singh, New Delhi
Shri Inderjit Singh, Chandigarh
Late Shri R.K. Dutta Gupta, New Delhi
Shri Amrik Singh, New Delhi
Shri Ranjit Singh, Patiala
Shri Sondeep Shankar, New Delhi
Shri J.C. Arora, New Delhi

THE PRIVATE COLLECTORS
Shri S.S. Hitkari, New Delhi
Bhai Suchet Singh, village Bhai Rupa, Moga, Punjab
Shri Atamjit Singh Vegha, Dehradun
Bhai Rattan Singh, village Daroli Bhai, Moga, Punjab
Shri Balbir Singh Singh, Jora Sahib Nangal, Faridkot, Punjab
Smt. Kumkum Singh, New Delhi
Shri Makkan Singh, Punjab and Sind Bank, New Delhi
Shri O.S. Chowdhary, Imperial Hotel, New Delhi
Shri Harish Chander Sharma, Chamba, H.P.

INSTITUTIONS
National Museum, New Delhi
Govt. Museum and Art Gallery, Chandigarh
Department of Culture, Archaeology and Archives, Govt. of Punjab, Chandigarh
Maharaja Ranjit Singh Museum, Amritsar
Sheesh Mahal Museum, Patiala
Qila Mubarak, Patiala
Bhai Vir Singh Sadan, New Delhi
Punjab and Sind Bank, New Delhi
Archaeological Survey of India, New Delhi
Baba Baghel Singh Museum, Bangla Sahib Gurdwara, New Delhi
State Museum, Shimla, Himachal Pradesh
Central Sikh Museum, Golden Temple, Amritsar
Patiala Archives, Patiala
Baba Farid Museum, Faridkot, Punjab
Lahore Museum, Lahore, Pakistan
Victoria and Albert Museum, London, UK

SPECIAL THANKS
Shri P.S. Aujala, Chandigarh
Shri S.S. Sheikhon, Chandigarh
Shri Piyara Singh, Chandigarh
Shri Mohan Singh, Patiala
Shri J.S. Anand, New Delhi
Dr. Maheep Singh, New Delhi
Dr. Mohinder Singh, New Delhi
Dr. Saifur Rehman Dar, Lahore, Pakistan
Miss Rajeshwari Shah, New Delhi